MW01268228

# Praise for *No Matter What, We Keep Dancing*

"Hannah's was an extraordinary life and how fortunate so many of us are to have known her as our teacher and friend. In my case - for more than 50 years. Hannah's story is one of history and relationships. Moreover, it is the story of how passion and dedication to dance and to teaching gave Hannah resilience that she in turn gifted to all of those she touched. In this book, the author uses first-hand accounts from Hannah's diaries to bring this inspirational story to life. As I read each vignette, I hear Hannah's voice and the lessons she taught me. In one section, where she describes what it felt like when she first arrived in America, she says: "So much to see and so much to learn." Those were words Hannah lived by and modeled for us. The author begins the book describing her Mother as a storyteller. So too is Evelyn Summer. This compelling book is told with love and sensitivity and I couldn't stop turning the pages for more."

*Judy Jablon*
*Executive Director, Leading for Children*
*Early Childhood Consultant*
*Former Student and Friend of Hannah Kroner*

I have had the good fortune of knowing Hannah Kroner, the subject of No Matter What, We Keep Dancing and Evelyn Summer, her daughter and the author. Getting to know them and being inspired by Hannah as a person and by her story, I am delighted that Evelyn's writing and the collection of poignant photos allow the reader to come along experiencing the journey as a fellow traveler.

What makes the book inspirational is Hannah, a Jewish victim of Nazi terror whose indomitable spirit overcomes harrowing danger and hardship. Throughout it all, she remained faithful to her raison d'être of being a dancer and a dance instructor. Along the way and over many years, she – through dance – radiates grace, class and a contagious joy that inspires her students and enriches their lives.

*That joy awaits the reader of this book.*

*James Muyskens*
*Former President, Queens College, CUNY*
*University Professor, Graduate Center, CUNY*

"*No Matter What, We Keep Dancing* is a moving and important memoir that tells the story of Hannah Kroner, a holocaust survivor. It is a story about family, loyalty, friendship, love and a passion for dance that sustained Hannah through life's most difficult moments. I was touched and inspired by her story. This ultimately uplifting memoir shows the strength and generosity of one woman who impacted the lives of many, both during her lifetime and through her legacy. The dancers and teachers who she trained continue to spread her positive message of believing in oneself, working hard and giving to others as the path to a happy and accomplished life. I was fortunate to be one of the lucky students that she taught in her dance studio and blessed to be able to call her a friend."

*JoAnne Greenbaum*
*Lecturer and Coordinator, Postsecondary Reading and Learning*
*Certificate Program*
*California State University, Fullerton*

"Talent, perseverance, commitment, and passion triumphed over persecution and rejection. That is the legacy of Holocaust survivor, dancer, performer, and dance teacher Hannah Kroner. Her life begins in Berlin in 1920, an adored and talented daughter of the Kroners. Already at an early age she exhibits exceptional talent for dance and music. She is accepted as a student by Max Terpis, the famed Director of the Berlin Opera Ballet Company and the head of a prominent dance school in Berlin. When Germany elected Adolf Hitler as their Chancellor, Terpis continued to teach her, even though it was prohibited. She felt isolated since she could not participate in any public functions with her Aryan school mates. In 1936, she became part of the Jewish Cultural Society (Kulturbund) in Germany as a performer and choreographer. As the persecution of Jews continued in Germany the Kroners sailed to America in 1939. After a career in nightclubs, marriage and two children, she began to teach dance in her living room to friends and neighbors' children. This eventually led her to establish a prestigious dance school in Queens and ultimately Albertson, NY, that continues 70 years later as the legacy of Hannah Kroner. Evelyn Summer, her daughter, has written a warm and beautiful memoir chronicling her mother's extraordinary life and accomplishments. A tribute to a great lady; read it and enjoy it!"

*Irving Roth*
*Holocaust Resource Center-Temple Judea of Manhasset*

# NO MATTER WHAT,
# WE KEEP DANCING

# NO MATTER WHAT,

# WE KEEP DANCING

## HANNAH KRONER'S LEGACY

## EVELYN SUMMER

Yellow Rose Publishing Company

For permission requests, please address:
The Yellow Rose Publishing Company
1805 215th street
Bayside, NY 11360

Published 2017 by The Yellow Rose Publishing Company
Printed in the United States of America

19 18 17   1 2 3 4

ISBN: 978-0-9986228-0-4
Library of Congress Control Number: 2017931507

# DEDICATION

This book is dedicated to my mother, Hannah Kroner Segal, who inspired me through her courage, persistence, creativity, and intelligence.

# TABLE OF CONTENTS

## PART I — THE DANCER

## PART II — THE TEACHER

## PART III — LEGACY

# INTRODUCTION

My mother was a storyteller. Throughout her lifetime, she collected those stories and shared them with her family and friends. As a child, she tucked me into bed with tales about her school days, special German foods she loved, and most of all about her years as a dancer. During my childhood those conversations took place at the beach, on walks, in our living room, and at our dinner table. There were also stories about the Holocaust, the fears she had that her father would be taken away, just because they were Jewish. She talked about her boyfriend Vimms and her girlfriend Susanne, who I felt a personal connection to.

There were talks about her life in America as a dancer and the dancing school she founded in 1947. One day she opened a wooden box and slowly lifted the cover to reveal a faded yellow rose she kept for over 50 years, given to her by her dance teacher. I learned that this color represents love, friendship, sympathy, and caring. She told me about how it came to be her special flower that her students presented to her at the end of performances for almost seventy years.

In addition to our discussions, she wrote lengthy letters and cards to friends in Europe and in America. During the last two decades of her life, she participated in writing groups where she stored her memories in spiral notebooks. She passed away at the age of 95, leaving a treasure trove. Now, through her writing and conversations, I share her extraordinary life as she told it to me.

# PART 1

# THE DANCER

# CHAPTER I – GROWING UP IN BERLIN

The sun rose into the sky as my mother Hannah Kroner Segal and I climbed the familiar steps onto the warm sands of Cape Cod. She carried a striped beach umbrella and I followed with our chairs. On this summer morning in 1991, I felt the sadness that hung over us. It was our first summer without my father. Although I visited them here over the years, this felt different.

The chairs and umbrella were opened and we sat down, gazing at the quiet bay. I remembered how much I loved to listen to her stories when I was a young girl, learn about her childhood in Berlin, Germany during the twenties and thirties, feel as if I knew some of the friends and family she spoke about personally. During the following week at the Cape, the stories flowed and I treasured each one, hoping to share them with my husband and two sons. "Mom," I said, "you have many memories of such an important time, can you write them down for me?" She agreed and so her writing journey began. The notebooks filled up over the next 20 years, telling the stories of her family; the tumultuous experiences they endured. There were also memories of happier moments; her career, wedding, birth of her children, and so much more. She lived to the age of 95, continuing to write and left a magnificent gift that I recently began to unwrap;

"*During the summer in Berlin, my father and I took our customary Sunday morning stroll through the park. We found a sheltered little opening and he sat down on the bench. 'Can we play mother and child?' I asked. Smilingly he nodded. I collected some leaves and grass, pretended to cook it on a stove and served it to him in my cupped hand. 'Here is your spinach,' I said, 'eat it all up!' He pretended to eat, quickly dropping the leaves by the side. 'Don't do that,' I protested, 'spinach is healthy.' And imitating my mother at the dinner table, 'empty your plate, or you can't play.' My patient loving father obliged and ate some of the grass. I was satisfied and we continued our walk. Memories of my father all center around this love, sense of humor, and patience for me, his only child, born after ten years of marriage when he was already 47 years old. My mother was 15 years younger and they waited until after World War I to start their family.*

*On our Sunday walks he loved to tell me how much he wanted to become a concert pianist. His father, a doctor, would not permit this choice, expecting him to study medicine or law as his brothers did. Stubbornly he did neither but founded a wholesale business of women's wear which became very successful until Hitler came to power and closed all Jewish owned businesses.*"

My grandmother, Granny as I called her, was a resilient, strong-minded person. In my mother's notebooks she wrote about this woman who would play a key part in their survival:

"*'Is Mom home?' was always my first question after running up the stairs to our third floor apartment in Berlin at the end of a school day. She was a strict mother and expected discipline and perfection from me, her only child. She was also the most comforting and understanding person. I knew without a doubt that I was the most important person in my mother's life and that she would shield and defend me against anything bad that might occur. She was 32 years old when I came along.*

*Blessed with enormous strength and determination, which eventually saved our lives, she was a very devoted and support-ive wife. In 1926 Germany experienced a depression which damaged my father's business of wholesale women's wear enormously. My mother and our nanny started to manufacture down comforters and pillows in our house and sold them to neighbors and friends. It provided a very helpful income for our family."*

My mother often took her heavy brown photo album off the shelf and pointed to her baby pictures taken soon after she was born on May 22nd, 1920. There were photos of vacations with my grandparents, Elsa and Eugene Kroner; to Paris, Switzerland, and the North Sea;

*"With the end of World War 1, the custom of spending July away from the hot city happily resumed. Two months after my birth, wrapped in warm blankets, I was taken along by my parents and my nanny to the seashore. A then fashionable summer resort at the Baltic Sea, called Arendsee was selected. I have been told that I was a well behaved baby and have to assume that my ever present love for beaches and the ocean must have started at that time!"*

"Over the next five years...Old photos show my parents in elegant attire promenading on the boardwalk, proudly holding my hand, with a watchful Nanny nearby. The afternoons were quite special. We would dress up and visit the Strand Café by the beach. There was cake with mountains of whipped cream and an orchestra providing background music.

As I grew older my parents took me to Braubach, a little rural town in the south of Germany. In some of the neighboring towns violin makers had settled and had established quite a reputation for excellence, second only to the Italians. For some time, I had asked for violin lessons and now I got a big happy surprise. My mother bought me a well-built violin and I was in seventh heaven. I took it to bed with me every night and started lessons when we returned to Berlin.

*We had planned to travel to Switzerland. One morning big headlines in the local papers announced a crisis for the Austrian banks. My parents seemed very worried and my father raced to the bank to change all his Austrian money into a safer currency before the banks were closed altogether. I remember feeling scared and insecure and so it was decided to cancel the last week and return home."*

What my mother remembered was an event that affected much of the world. After the First World War and the termination of the Austro-Hungarian Empire, the main bank in Austria continued to try to do business as usual. Bank practices led to a financial imbalance. Bank regulations became weaker. By 1931, the government's trustworthiness came into question. The panic in the city of Vienna brought down banks in Amsterdam and Warsaw, spread to Germany, and ultimately to the United States which was already in the Great Depression since 1929. The Nazi Party placed the blame for the economic problems and unemployment on the Jews as well as the Versailles Treaty. This gave the people an enemy they could blame for all their difficulties:

*"In 1930 the July destination was to be a seaside resort on the Belgium coast. I had started French in school, and this would*

*be a chance to practice the language...I proudly read the French menus for all the meals, ordered in French, and conversed with the hotel staff and my little girlfriends. The reward for this accomplishment was to add a week in Paris! I was jubilant! Going up the Eiffel Tower, my nanny stayed on the ground to catch me in case I would fall down, which I found both touching and silly. At the Louvre I tried to imitate the smile of the Mona Lisa and was really upset that the beautiful Venus de Milo had lost one arm. I shall be forever grateful to my parents for having given me a wealth of experience, learning, comparing, and evaluating life styles, never to be forgotten."*

In addition to violin, swimming, and ice-skating lessons, she was also given ballet lessons at a young age. My grandparents couldn't possibly know that her growing love of dance would ultimately save their lives. During my mother's early years, she met a little girl who would become her best friend:

*"Her name was Susanne Wachsner. We entered school as classmates. She lost her mother at a very young age and lived with her father...Our teacher gave us seats in order of our marks and Susanne and I always wound up as numbers two and three, alternately. Number one was a very bright girl, Miriam Meyer, who retained the first place in our class forever. Well, Susanne and I became very close friends as we moved into high school and then at age 16 she lost her father. So my mother took her into our family and we felt like real sisters."*

Hannah and Susanne

During our days in Cape Cod, my mother's stories continued. "Mom," I began, "tell me again what happened to you at school when Hitler came to power?" Lifting her eyes to the blue sky, she answered:

> *"I befriended Greta, a pretty girl with long, blonde pigtails. Her father was a former army officer, who had joined the Nazi Party early. One day in 1933, Greta informed me that she could not visit me anymore since she was not permitted to be friends with Jewish girls."*

My mother added that she told her parents and asked the question, WHY? They hugged her silently.

There was another vacation that remained in her memory:

> *"In 1934, my family and I spent our summer vacation at a seaside resort in the north of Germany. As we left the beach to return to our hotel, we heard the voices of newspaper vendors, 'President Hindenburg has chosen Adolf Hitler as the new President and his successor as the leader of the new German Reich!'*

*My parents stopped dead in their tracks, looked at each other and said, 'This is not good for us.' I was still far too young to understand what gave them so much reason to worry. Well, Hitler did become the head of the New Germany and the world soon found out what the consequences were to be for Europe, America, and in our case, very quickly the German Jews!"*

The lives of the Germans changed completely when Adolf Hitler became chancellor and then merged that with the presidency of Germany after Paul von Hindenburg died in August 1934. He also became commander of the army and immediately suspended the basic rights of the people. Hitler thus became the dictator of Germany. There were death sentences for sabotage, and arson. Citizens were sentenced to prison without a trial or an attorney. The guarantees under the Weimar democracy were destroyed. There were other laws that were specifically against the Jews. They included the restriction of students at schools and universities and the denial of admission to medical schools. Jewish doctors were not reimbursed by state health insurance and in the city of Munich they couldn't treat non-Jewish patients. Jewish lawyers were forbidden to work on legal matters in Berlin.

As Jews, my mother and her parents were affected in many ways. My grandfather lost many of his customers because Jewish owned businesses were being boycotted. The lives of the Jews changed as Hitler came to power:

*"Jews lost their jobs, businesses and practices. Jewish doctors were only allowed to treat Jewish patients. Business owners from small retail stores to large factories had to turn over their long established successful businesses to non-Jewish employees. - without compensation. Performers: movie, theater, and opera, even the most famous, had to stop working in their professions. Theater and films had to be 'Judenrein' (free from Jews) and so the well-known artists immediately left the country, trying to find work in foreign cities. Internationally known movie and stage stars found work fairly soon in Hollywood, London, Paris, and Vienna."*

Among those who fled Europe were Otto Klemperer, Andre Previn, Marlene Dietrich, Hedy Lamar, Peter Lorre, Roman Polanski, and Otto Preminger. They became well known artists in America. In addition to the Jews, there were others who were persecuted, among them the disabled, homosexuals, Socialists, Polish, and Jehovah's Witnesses.

At the same time across the ocean, about 15,000 people came together in New York to protest the Nazis. Ten years later in 1943 over 30,000 held a rally in Madison Square Garden in New York City with the cry of "Stop Hitler Now!"

Despite all the restrictions, my mother and her parents along with many other Jews, continued to live their daily lives. It became an increasingly dangerous time for them. My mother told me about one of those moments. She and her girlfriend Susanne were walking down a large avenue in Berlin during a parade. Soldiers marched down the streets and huge crowds gathered to watch. As the marchers came closer, she noticed that the people raised their right arms in a salute and shouted, "Heil Hitler!" Immediately the two girls ducked into a store and waited until the parade ended. She told me that they could have been arrested for not joining in.

At the age of thirteen, her life became much more difficult. Her notebooks reveal how she kept her spirits up;

> "The world of dance studies became my refuge through the support of my teachers Max Terpis and Rolf Arco. Max Terpis was born and educated in Switzerland. He moved to Germany in the 1920s to study dance. This led to a most successful career as the director of the Berlin Opera Ballet Company and the head of a very prominent school of dance. In this school, I was fortunate enough to be accepted as a student just before the start of the Hitler years. This involved ten classes a week in all forms of dance and extra hours of practicing. We also had classes in mime, improvisation, and choreography, had to play an instrument, read music scores, design costumes, and write ballet plots. This special teacher did not confine himself to just teaching dance! He observed our strength and shortcomings and steered

*us into the most successful way to achieve our goal, without discouraging us in the process. Discovering my ability to teach, choreograph dances, and coach younger students, he gave me opportunities for practice in those areas, laying the groundwork for my teaching career as well as performing and company choreography.*

Hannah's Dance Class

*But maybe more important for me as a Jew was the fact that this Swiss National detested Hitler and his regime and refused to follow the orders to expel Jewish students from his school. He protected me and two others from feeling like persecuted under-dogs. He also boosted my self-esteem by pointing out that I was very fortunate to be able to use music by Jewish composers and authors while the German Culture was dragged down by the exclusion of all those wonderful Jewish artists. To this day, a lifetime later, I still have my notebooks with his dances, enabling me to recreate some of his work for my own students."*

From Hannah's Dance Notebook

One friend in her dance class became a special part of her life:

*"The year was 1934, I met Trudel one day in dancing school. She had come to Berlin from Mannheim in the south of Germany to study dance at this prestigious school. We took an immediate liking to each other and when she was looking for a furnished room, my mother offered her to move into a spare room in our apartment. That started a very close friendship in spite of the fact that she was seven years older than I. It had taken her several years of secretarial work to save enough money to fulfill her dream. The fact that she came from a Catholic family made living with us, a Jewish family, quite risky under Hitler's laws. But she couldn't have cared less. A warm, loving, and compassionate person, she was also very creative. That winter, our dancing school had a costume party and Trudel cast us as a married couple from the countryside. The idea was to avoid being recognized by anyone before midnight. Trudel, slim and petite, dressed as a little old man, wig, beard, mask, and all. I was going to be the wife, in a very full dress, with extra padding to disguise my figure, a wig, and special mask covering my*

*entire face. But we both did not realize that the mask had only a tiny opening for the mouth. I was stuck until midnight without food. My friend found a way. She kept pushing raisins through the mouth to keep me from starving! My only consolation was that no one recognized me, not even our teacher who danced with me, still puzzled who I was. A triumph for Trudel!*

*After two years of having her in our family this situation became too dangerous for her. So she auditioned for and was accepted as a dancer in the theater of a small town. I was heartbroken at this separation, even though she promised to visit us whenever possible. She kept her word and spent many hours on trains to visit us for just a few precious hours, before returning to her performances and rehearsals.*

*After we left Germany, Trudel, violently anti-Nazi, swore she would also leave this barbaric country. True to her conviction, she met a French prisoner of war who was assigned to backstage duties of her theater and married him after the war. They lived in France for the rest of their lives.*

*One year, attending class on my birthday we all got dressed hurriedly to go out to a celebration. Terpis found out the reason for this unusual haste, and quickly went into his study to come out with one yellow rose for me! I treasured that flower, preserved it, and brought it with me to the USA. My own students, upon learning this story, have made the yellow rose my special flower at all occasions!"*

The yellow rose represents friendship, sympathy, respect and compassion. It symbolizes eternal friendship.

The Holocaust laws affected her life in her precious dance world:

> "Two sisters in my dance class, whose father belonged to the Nazi party, spread the word in our school that Terpis was still teaching Jewish students and should be stopped. The order came; 'Stop teaching Jews or we'll close your school.' Terpis called the entire student body and teachers into the studio and announced, 'I am a Swiss National and not subject to German law personally. If Hannah has to leave, I shall close my school and return to Switzerland. You can all find some other suitable teacher.' There was total silence in the room and then one by one they declared total agreement with his position and assured me that I had nothing to fear. The sisters left the school. None of them could foresee what was to come."

She continued to study at Terpis' school as Hitler and the Nazis enacted new laws that especially targeted the Jews:

> "I had many good friends in my class but I started to feel very lonely and excluded as time went on. There were class trips to theaters and dance concerts, to museums and special films, but Jews were no longer permitted to enter any of those places so I could not join these activities. My school friends held birthday parties and social gatherings in restaurants but again I was not allowed to enter these public places. It started to feel like a noose around my neck, which was pulled tighter from day to day."

It was 1936 and the Olympics were held in Berlin. During those weeks, the Nazis even removed their "Jews Unwelcome" from some of the public areas. It was Hitler's plan to show the entire world that the Aryan people were the dominant race. Jesse Owens, an African American, proved him wrong by becoming the most successful athlete of the 1936 Berlin Games sealing his place in Olympic history.

A year before, the Nazis announced new laws known as the Nuremburg Laws that deprived the Jews of many rights. Anyone who had more than two Jewish grandparents was defined as a Jew, so that those who had converted to Christianity could be declared as being Jewish. They included some Protestant ministers, nuns, and Catholic priests. The laws included the prohibition of marriage to anyone with "German blood." They also lost the right to vote:

> "We German Jews felt somewhat safer during the Olympic weeks. The Nazis had temporarily suspended their persecution of the Jews, not wanting to risk these activities while all countries were represented in Berlin. The city was crowded with foreign visitors and athletes. I noticed that most of them wore pins with the flags of their countries on their lapels. The American flag was of special interest to me with hopes and prayers to be able some future day to also wear one. The little lapel pins were seen also in the store window of jewelry stores and I was tempted to buy one. But the laws stated that one had to show one's passport when purchasing one."

Many Jews in Germany had already left by this time for other countries. The laws became more unbearable, physical violence and legal repression increased. Jews were dismissed from civil service jobs and their businesses were boycotted by public policy. More were beginning to plan their departure. They depended on other countries being willing to take them. The German government placed a large emigration tax on the Jews and restricted the amount of money that they could transfer out of German banks. No one could imagine how many more liberties would be denied during the next months and years.

# CHAPTER 2 – THE JUDISCHE KULTURBUND

My mother left school at 16 to devote all her energies to achieving her dream to dance in a company. She wrote:

> *"My class was considered performance ready, and most of my classmates found jobs as dancers on the stage and in the movies. I was heartbroken, ready and able to perform but prevented from employment on any stage as a Jew. I started to do some solo performances at various Jewish community functions and then joined a dance company that did some local performances. I was hoping to get bookings to Italy and Switzerland. One of the dancers I met in this group also danced at the theater of the Jewish Kulturbund, in Berlin."*

From its start in 1933, founded by Kurt Singer, a German Jewish doctor and music director, the Judische Kulturbund (Jewish Theater) became a safe haven for Jews who were fired due to the Civil Service laws. This also gave them an income. It reduced any social unrest. The Nazis supported the theater as proof to the rest of the world that the Jews were not being treated poorly. Thousands of artists performed in the Berlin Kulturbund and in over forty other theaters throughout

Germany until 1941 when the last one in Berlin was closed and the performers taken to concentration camps:

*"The history and story of this most important organization of Jewish culture was that it permitted and in fact was ordered by the Nazi regime to function as a showcase of the 'humane treatment' of the Jews by Hitler'".*

She wrote about how she was accepted into this theater:

*"The year was 1936, the Kulturbund was playing an operetta Die Czardas Fuerstein and my friend being one of the dancers, had heard that a member of the ballet was leaving. She suggested that I should become the replacement. In two short dance rehearsals I had to learn the various dances and stand in the wings of the stage for two nights to observe and learn all the things the dancers had to do besides dancing. I was very excited about this chance to finally be in a theater. My recollection of that first month as a member to the company is sheer happiness, without any sense of danger. The drawbacks were such things as the fact that my beloved dancing teacher, as a non-Jew, was unable to enter the theater to see me, as were my non-Jewish dancer friends. Also the theater was on the opposite end of the city from where I lived and went to school so that a lot of time was spent travelling by subway to and from rehearsals and evening performances...The next production I was needed for was the opera Eugene Onegin and so for one month of performances I was in my glory. We enjoyed the backstage life in our dressing room and I spent a good deal of the time when I was not on stage in the wings, learning the score and watching the singers. But slowly, little changes occurred. People would leave Germany and new faces would be on stage. The talk backstage changed from 'when is the next rehearsal' to 'have you heard from the consulate 'or 'which country will still admit us?'...I too had come to realize that I must leave Germany and so I had written letters to all the theaters in Switzerland and Scandinavia, applying for a job as a dancer with good personal recommendations by*

*my Swiss teacher. Ironically all the answers stated that although I could not perform as a Jew in Germany, I also could not perform as a German in the other countries. I was devastated. My mother had already established contact with some cousins in the USA who were willing to send us an affidavit, which was necessary for entrance into America. My parents felt that America was too far to let me go alone, and applied for entry visa for all three of us. I am eternally grateful that I did not find employment in Switzerland in which case my parents would have stayed in Berlin and surely perished, this initial disappointment actually saved their lives.*

Program from the Kulturbund

*I continued my work at the theatre. Somehow when the curtain went up, we all on stage were in the happy world of make-believe. Not so during rehearsals. By now everyone saw the urgency to get out of Germany and the talk centered on this topic. Of course there were also some optimists. One of the singers would always tell me, 'you will all be sorry that you have left! But I will remain here and some day, when everything is back to normal here, I shall be the one who will send you an affidavit to return to Berlin!"*

17

Her experiences in the Kulturbund were included in several books including *Premiere und Pogrom* by E. Geisel and H. Broder. "It was a very tense, nervous time. At the stage entrance, the Secret Police was posted to watch who entered or left the theatre. My parents were worried that they would grab us from the stage when the last performance of our ballet was done. One of our close friends, non-Jewish and purposely dressed to look like a 'real German woman' from the lower working class, hung around the stage entrance every night, grabbed me as soon as I came out of the door and brought me home by subway." (Translated)

Over the years, I heard about the generous cousins who saved my mother and grandparents' lives:

> "The year was 1918, the World War was over. My parents lived in Berlin, trying to return to a fairly normal life. My father got a letter from the USA. A cousin, May Friedman who lived in Sioux City, Iowa, was planning a visit with a girlfriend to Berlin and needed an English speaking tour guide. Could he be of help? As it happened my mother spoke English fluently, having been born to a German Jewish father and a British mother, who was raised in London. So May and her friend arrived and my mother offered to show her around. The two American girls were very grateful for that, and never forgot this Berlin visit.
>
> The years went by, Jews faced concentration camps and death, or if lucky, emigration to another country. Most of the other countries were not very hospitable to the immigrants, or just refused them entry. The US was willing to accept persecuted Jews but only if an American citizen guaranteed five years of financial support, if needed. My father optimistically thought that Hitler would go away again and was inclined to stay in Berlin, the city of his birth. My mother saw 'no future' for me in that country anymore and wrote to Cousin May who now lived in Kansas City, Missouri, with a plea to at least let me come over to pursue my dance career. Immediately came a reply and the necessary papers to guarantee my support and my parents. Well, we were lucky."

As a child, I always looked forward to our summer vacation in New London, Connecticut. There were daily trips to Ocean Beach where my mother would tell my brother and me stories. One of those was about her driving lessons:

> *"My 18ᵗʰ birthday! My only wish for a present; driving lessons! My parents were hesitant. This was Hitler Germany and Jews were not allowed anymore to own a car. So why learn to drive at this dangerous time? I had the answer. 'We are waiting for our immigration papers for the USA and it would be an asset for me to be able to drive already in our new country!' My parents gave in and we looked for a driving school, still willing to teach Jews. Friends recommended a teacher who took this risk and was courageous enough to accept me as a student. My best friend Susanne also enrolled and both of us enjoyed our lessons in a small, blue four cylinder Opel. Finally, our teacher considered us ready to take the test for the license but warned us that the Nazi inspectors would be extra tough on us! Susanne was tested first and made a small mistake during a turn, she was reprimanded very rudely by the inspector. Losing her composure, she gave a wisecrack as an answer, and was immediately told that she had failed her test. Now it was my turn behind the wheel and my heart beat into my throat. But I was able to keep calm and concentrate on the task at hand, finishing the test without any mishap. I received my license a few days later and was stunned to see a big red letter 'J' printed on it. This would quickly identify me everywhere as a Jew and make driving in Germany too dangerous to even try."*

One evening as she rehearsed for a performance at the Kulturbund, her life changed once more. She wrote:

> *"The year was 1938, November 9ᵗʰ. We heard crashing glass outside, sirens and screams. It was the infamous Kristallnacht (Night of Broken Glass.) My mother called and told my dance teacher to send me home immediately, that synagogues were burning and that she didn't want me to be clear across Berlin,*

*and I should come home. My teacher said to immediately get dressed and get home. I was scared and started to cry, it was very traumatic. So I saw stores, glass on the street and I started to run pretty much home."*

A Polish Jew living in Paris, shot a German Embassy official after hearing that his parents who lived in Germany were deported and denied re-entry into Poland. As revenge, rioters all over Germany smashed the windows of about 1,400 synagogues, and Jewish owned stores. Mobs roamed through the night and attacked Jews. About 30,000 Jewish men were arrested and taken to concentration camps. Most were released during the next few months if they would make arrangements to leave Germany, which was almost impossible because only a limited number of countries would accept them. The government blamed the Jews and fined them about four hundred million dollars. Their homes were confiscated as part of the fines.

My grandfather escaped detection by hiding out in the park overnight, along with many of the men. It was a long, scary night for all the Jews:

*"The next morning I joined the Kulturbund for a rehearsal. A colleague came running over to me. 'Hannah, I know you are waiting to get to America! There is a long line at the American Consulate. They are all hoping to get waiting numbers for visas! Get over there quickly!' I phoned my parents and my father rushed over to line up. 'Wait,' I told my father, 'my best friend Susanne also has an affidavit for the United States. She should come to get into this line!' My father raced to a public phone and called Susanne, luckily at home. He told her to come quickly. Well she did but it took about half an hour to get from her house to the street we were at. Once more, fate stepped in to touch our lives. She reached the line an hour later, about 100 spaces behind us. Finally, we moved forward and my father and I got the papers to enter the US. A few places after us the line was stopped and the consulate closed. My friend was left among the group still waiting outside. The visa number required our family to wait for a whole year before being allowed to leave Germany.*

21

*It became a question of what would come first, deportation to concentration camps or permission to enter the land of freedom. My father couldn't work any longer, we sold our furniture to buy food and pay rent. I was still performing in our Jewish Kulturbund theater and in love with Vimms, second violinist of the orchestra. One day he gave me a present, crafted out of a stone, it was a red scarab on a gold chain. Shortly after, another law was passed, all Jews were told to go to their neighborhood school and turn in all their gold and silver jewelry and other items. Failure to do that would result in arrest and deportation to a concentration camp. I hated to turn in this precious gift, so lovingly made. My mother had a good idea. She asked a jeweler to take off the gold part and turn it in, leaving me the handmade part I kept it throughout my life."*

Hannah and Vimms
(Joseph Schecter)

*Vimms too was waiting for a visa to America, but also had Norwegian citizenship that kept him safe as a Jew in Germany. After Kristallnacht, he decided that the time had come to return to Norway and await entry to the USA there, in safety rather than risk remaining in Berlin! He proposed to marry me and take me with him. We would then both deal with the American Consulate in Oslo, while my parents would await their entry visa in Berlin. Hopefully we would all be reunited in New York before too long. I thought that was a great idea but my parents did not share my enthusiasm. He left Berlin a few days later and I shall never forget our goodbyes at the airport. In Norway he right away applied for entry to USA, expecting a few months waiting time. "*

What neither of them knew was that just four months later, on April 8th to 9th, 1940, Germany invaded Norway. Vidkun Quisling became the Prime minister as King Haakon V11 escaped to London. About 1,700 Jews lived in Norway at that time. Arrests took place a year later after the German invasion of the Soviet Union. About 900 Jews were able to escape to Neutral Sweden through the efforts of Norwegian police and members of the underground. Norwegian church leaders protested but deportations continued. Other Jews went into hiding. More than 750 Jews were deported and most of them were murdered in Auschwitz. After the German forces in Norway surrendered to Allies on May 8, 1945, Quisling was arrested and found guilty of treason. He was executed on October 24, 1945. Hannah wrote:

*"I never heard from Vimms again and all attempts after the war to learn about his fate were unsuccessful."*

She never forgot the day her teacher Max Terpis called her into his office;

> *"With tears in his eyes he told me that his school would be closed if he would continue to teach Jews. He was very angry and bitter and promised to close up anyway and return to Switzerland rather than go against his convictions.*
>
> *One of his former pupils, who knew me, had opened a dance studio in another part of the city. She allowed me, at great personal risk, to come and practice whenever it was empty so that I could continue to train and exercise, as dancers must do. I had to walk along the street, wait until it was empty and quickly enter her studio not to be spotted by a neighbor or the janitor who would report both of us to the secret police with terrible consequences. I was told to look at the window shades, if they were up, I could go inside, if they were drawn, it was not safe and I was to go home.*
>
> *Once inside none of us talked until pillows were put over the telephone and window shutters closed. The pianist of Terpis' school came secretly to play the piano for me and help me rehearse a solo repertoire for America. These two women helped me at the risk of their lives, which I have never forgotten."*

As her family waited anxiously through the long months, my mother prepared for the career she hoped to pursue in America. Her teacher wrote a testimonial for her. It read in part:

"...She has gained an exceptional knowledge of the classical ballet, modern technic, and character... which enable her to accept any position as professional dancer. She has a special talent for pedagogic (teaching). Her clear forethought and her quiet authority, proved herself well capable of being a good teacher..." Max Terpis

Fritz Wisten of the Judische Kulturbund also wrote:

"Miss Hannah Kroner was employed as dancer and figurante in our operas, operettas, and pantomimes from August 1937...Her main talent referred to the choreographic training of dancers...In our pantomime 'The Elopement' performed in August 1939, Miss Kroner was entrusted with the choreographic coaching."

These papers were brought to America, and kept in her closet, as reminders of a past she lived through. Now I handled each yellowed sheet as if it were a precious flower, to be preserved to tell the story of this unbelievable time.

Following Kristallnacht, Jewish organizations such as the Kulturbund were ordered to close, but with other countries reacting to the violence and the repressive actions, the Nazis told the organizations to remain open. They also released the performers from concentration camps. There had been orders during Kristallnacht not to set fire to the Kulturbund theater. Kristallnacht was an event that the rest of the world condemned. Yet immigration to many countries was restricted, trapping the remaining Jews in Germany. They now realized that violence could result and that most of western civilization was apathetic to this horror. One of the few that did increase their immigration of Jews was England. Kristallnacht was the beginning of the Nazis' plans for the 'Final Solution' that would result in the murder of 6,000,000.

At the same time as my mother waited for their visa number to come up, a ship filled with 937 mostly German Jews sailed from France, heading for Cuba. It was the St. Louis. These refugees didn't know that a few days before they left, a massive anti-Semitic rally with 40,000 Cubans sought to stop the passengers from debarking. While the ship waited in the harbor, negotiations failed and a few days later, the St. Louis was ordered to leave Cuba. The United States had a strict immigration quota and wouldn't admit them either. So the ship returned with Great Britain, France, Belgium, and The Netherlands who agreed to take the Jews. About half who returned to the continent survived the German invasion throughout Western Europe in 1940.

# CHAPTER 3 - COMING TO AMERICA

As the departure date drew closer, the suitcases were packed, filled with dance notes, photos of the family, professional dance photographs, costumes, sheet music, everything that would be needed for a new theatrical career in America:

> *"It was September 1939; we were booked on the SS Europa to leave Germany forever. We had moved into a boarding house for what we thought to be two weeks... Headlines: 'Germany invades Poland.' The Second World War had begun. We were stuck. Cousins in America secured passage via Holland on the SS Rotterdam for November."*

On the first of September as the tanks rolled into Poland, the Jews were immediately treated brutally. Even as they attempted to flee to the areas under Soviet control, the German invasion was so swift that hundreds of thousands were unable to escape.

My mother wrote about those dangerous weeks while they waited:

> *"For a Jew in Nazi Germany every additional day meant possible deportation. In October I had an attack of appendicitis*

*and again we did not know if we would be able to travel. Also, the Gestapo regularly inspected the boarding house and the owner was told to get rid of us. We had no kitchen privileges and food was now rationed. Jews were not permitted into restaurants and we depended on the help of friends to get meals.*

*While we waited, my friend Susanne decided to learn dress-making, considered practical for emigration. She was very successful and made a long black evening gown for me 'for America.'"*

Susanne                       Hannah with Susanne's Dress

That gown was to travel with my mother, destined to return to Berlin 73 years later.

Two months passed and on November 15th they finally boarded the train to Holland. Each was permitted to take ten German Marks out of the country, approximately forty dollars per person. Susanne accompanied them to the border. As they approached the station, there was an announcement;

*"All Jews through a gate to one side, the other passengers to remain. We walked through the gate, lining up for body search*

*by the Germans. A small booth, strip, be searched, get dressed, line up outside again. Suddenly an ear piercing scream from the other side. My girlfriend raced screaming toward the fence that divided us, her arms stretched out to my mother. Two Nazi guards grabbed her and pulled her back."*

They would never see each other again. Susanne ultimately perished. That moment remained with my mother throughout her life.

Hannah's Passport

Rotterdam was a different world than the one they had left. Rolls with butter and jam, eggs, chocolates! These were treats they had not seen for a long time. As in so much in her life, it was fate that they arrived in Holland in the winter of 1939. One week later they boarded their ship. That evening as they departed, everyone remained silent, lights were turned off. Would their ship sail through the mines planted in the English Channel by the Germans, ending their dreams of freedom? The long night finally ended peacefully. Ten days of blustery seas followed.

Unbeknownst to most everyone, in the spring of 1940, Nazi Germany invaded the Netherlands by bombing the Port of Rotterdam and threatening to do the same to other cities. Over a third of the port facilities were destroyed. By the end of 1945 about 78 percent of the Jews in the Netherlands were killed. Only 15,000 survived out of 150,000 who lived there in 1940. During the war, some Dutch citizens turned Jews over to the Nazis to collect a monetary reward while others were rescuers and hid Jews under threat of arrest. They included the courageous individuals who hid Anne Frank, her family, and friends.

Before their departure my mother rehearsed her dances in their home in Berlin. she was accompanied by her father on their grand piano:

> "My mother watched us and prodded him to slow down his tempo of Chopin's Minute Waltz so that I could properly dance to it. But he always insisted that the Minute Waltz had to be played in a minute, dancing or not!"

During their journey on the SS Rotterdam, she searched through her luggage in the storage area of the ship for her costumes to perform for the passengers, and lift their spirits:

> "I was asked by the captain to perform as part of the entertainment. So I danced and my father, familiar with my musical arrangements, proudly played the piano for me. I remember how stormy our trip was, both the dance floor and the grand piano swayed from side to side. 'If Mr. Chopin would be in my place now,' Dad commented with his usual dry sense of humor, 'he would have changed his composition to the Half-a-Minute Waltz!'"

Finally, their ship completed the arduous voyage across the Atlantic to America:

> "On the evening of the last day, as I gazed at the Statue of Liberty, my father held me tightly and said, 'Tonight we still have a bed with a roof over our head and good food. From tomorrow on we have to make a living in a strange country with a strange language.'"
>
> All we could see was a row of lights that looked like a chain of pearls which was, I guess, Brooklyn on one side and Staten Island on the other. There was a big big advertisement by Wrigley Chewing Gum. All people in Europe knew that the

*Americans were famous for their chewing gum and so when we saw the sign, we knew that there was really really the coast of this great big wonderful country that had given us refuge. So the excitement rose to a high pitch.*

*The next morning, we got up very early and the boat started to edge up and our line was pulling in, not Manhattan but across the river in Hoboken, New Jersey. Now people started to get very excited and they started to line up because these were the times when there was an island called Ellis Island which was, next to the concentration camps of Germany, the greatest horror of everybody. This was the place where people were taken who had not the right papers or had nobody to escort them from the boat. In those times you were not just allowed to leave the boat and come on land even if you had all the papers. We had of course cabled to our American relatives the boat on which we were arriving and since they lived in Kansas City, Missouri, they had arranged with some business acquaintances to be sure to get us off the boat.*

*As our turn came, our name was called and nobody stepped forward to escort us off the boat. We found out later that since our ship was delayed, they had gone to a restaurant for lunch. So we were denied admission to America and we had to step back. Here we were in complete despair, the Promised Land was so close and yet so far away and the danger of Ellis Island started to rear its head very large.*

*All of a sudden our name was called. A bellboy brought a message, it read, 'Welcome to America, I'm down here if you need me.' It was from a Dr. Hans Leipziger who had been our neighbor in Berlin, he and his family lived on the same floor. When he had to give up his apartment and couldn't practice anymore, we gave him permission to use some of our apartment for the time he was still in Berlin. He got out of Germany faster because he was put into concentration camp and his wife got papers very hurriedly for him and their daughter to leave. Once again it goes to show when one does something nice for people it is appreciated. When he heard we were coming, he made it his business to come to meet the boat. I think if anybody came close to look like an angel, he was the closest to having wings and floating down from Heaven that anybody could ever come. He came up and claimed us and here we were on American soil. I don't think anybody who hasn't lived through it can ever understand what it feels like to come from the country that will surely put you to death and then come into this big free wonderful country."*

On December 3rd, the New York Times reported that the Rotterdam "...was strictly a refugee ship...bearing 900 refugees from Germany...Few of the refugees spoke English but it was obvious from their sad eyes...that they had been through a good deal."

Throughout her life, my mother considered America to be the land of freedom. She told me that in Germany, everyone really thought that the streets were paved with gold!

Although there were reports about the horrifying events taking place in Europe, many could not comprehend what was happening. Even by 1943, the Allies took little action to help the Jews. The small country of Denmark however, did save almost all of their Jewish citizens.

Wannsee, Germany where the Nazis met to decide the "Final Solution" in 1943

On their first day in their new country, they explored New York City:

> *"So much to see and so much to learn. First a train ride into Manhattan from Hoboken, New Jersey. How to walk through a turnstile without getting stuck! How to sit on a subway seat without falling off in a curve. What narrow seats! We came out at 81st Street and walked over to Columbus Avenue, at that time under an old fashioned rather ugly elevated line. My mother felt 'everything in America is going to be beautiful.' We all got on a trolley car and rode down Broadway to Times Square. What an unbelievably exciting sight! In those years it still had glamour, and the theatre markers glistened in all colors. We walked a few blocks, totally overcome by this spectacle and had a hard time falling asleep later on, trying to understand that we were really here! We have arrived in New York, in the land of freedom of religion and from persecution. Coming from Hitler Germany and being alive and together, my parents and I were deeply grateful and relieved. Now we would start a new life in a brownstone on 84th Street."*

Many years later, Hannah wrote a poem about her experiences:

Coming from Europe
Our ship arrived early
New York was in view

Finally, I saw
The Statue of Liberty
Symbol of freedom

The coastline in view
Sparkled in brilliant sunshine
A precious jewel

We appreciate
Freedom only after it
Was taken away

As newly arrived immigrants my grandfather, now in his sixties, set out to find a job:

> *"Fate stepped in again as my father met a former business friend who was selling office supplies wholesale. He offered my father the chance to sell carbon paper, pencils and typewriter ribbons to offices in Manhattan. Dad jumped at this opportunity. He discovered one day that these items were sold at all the Woolworth stores for less money and promptly switched to buying there. I always felt that his customers felt sorry for him and therefore continued to use his services. It gave him back some self-esteem and made him the first breadwinner in our family. When I recall those times I marvel at the courage this former successful business owner needed to peddle pencils and papers in a new country with a different language and money system at an age when his contemporaries retired on Social Security."*

My grandmother's life also changed dramatically in America:

> *"From having been the lady of the house, with a maid and nanny in a very large apartment, she now lived in a one-bedroom residence in Manhattan, sleeping on a studio couch with a doily covering the orange crate night-table. Joining the ranks of factory workers, she started in a slipper factory, and then changed to Hanscom's Bakery where she was reprimanded by the forelady 'not to work so fast and spoil it for the other workers.' She adjusted to life in our new country with strength and great love. 'God bless America' was her favorite song and becoming an American citizen the most important day. When she passed away in 1970, she left a tremendous impact on our family. We often quote her expressions: 'Wenn schon, den schon' (if you do it, do it right.) 'Was andere knonnen, kann ich auch' (What others can do, I can do too,) and finally, 'Das soll so sein' (It's meant to be.) These are my memories of a very loving, caring, courageous, strong, and demanding woman."*

She kept birthday cards, theater programs, and letters from friends and family for over 70 years, in boxes, carefully organized. Seated on my sofa I opened and read some, different moments in her life sprang off the pages like a painting, vivid and inviting. Her notebooks revealed the beginning of her quest to perform in America:

*"I had arrived in New York! Having been trained as a professional dancer in Europe, able to do any type of dance, surely I would find work quickly. I walked down Broadway to Times Square, feeling confident and ready to launch my American career. Together with my parents, we entered a theater, later to become the home of David Letterman's show and purchased the cheapest seats. They were way up in the balcony but still close enough for us to see the lack of clothing on the dancers, not suitable for me to join. We realized this was burlesque!"*

I turned the pages, reading about what happened after that experience. She received a note with an audition date for the Corps de Ballet of the Metropolitan Opera:

*"With butterflies in my stomach, I found the stage door to that wonderful old building, a creaky old elevator took me up to the huge ballet rehearsal studio. After a short time which seemed to nervous me an eternity, the ballet master, Mr. Romanoff entered and introduced himself. We smiled at each other, and then discovered rather quickly that he spoke only Russian, and I spoke only German and some basic English. Fortunately, we found some common ground in the French ballet terminology. I tried my best, partially just guessing what he wanted to see. After 15 minutes of dancing, he smiled then shrugged his shoulders. Within seconds he was gone leaving me in despair. 'You will hear from us,' the secretary consoled me, pointing to the elevator. I understood! I did hear about one week later. A postcard told me that in December, the height of the winter season, the ballet company was filled, but that I showed enough promise and good training to be granted a scholarship to the opera school until a vacancy would occur, a good result, but I had to decline. As a new immigrant I had to find a paying job in show business, preferably also speaking English. There was a fringe benefit however, I was invited to meet a group of*

*dancers, also currently unemployed, they invited me to join their practice sessions. The dancers included Eugene Loring, who became well known in Hollywood, Michael Kidd who danced on Broadway, and Agnes DeMille, the renowned choreographer."*

Choreography of ballet in the American theater was dramatically influenced by Agnes DeMille through her first accomplishment; *Rodeo* in 1942. This was followed by the Broadway musical *Oklahoma* in 1943, which was the first time that dance was instrumental in moving the plot along. She continued to choreograph dances on Broadway in shows like *Carousel* and *Brigadoon*, as well as for the American Ballet Theater:

> *"Agnes de Mille had great courage, a delightful sense of humor and was not afraid to voice her opinion, I admired her greatly. It was one of the unfulfilled dreams of my life, not to have been in her dancing shoes."*

Seventy years later, my mother saw Agnes DeMille once more at a gala performance of the American Ballet Theater. As we sat in our plush red seats at Lincoln Center, this grand dancer was brought onto the stage to receive the honor she deserved.

My mother wrote about another experience she had looking for opportunities to perform:

> *"There was an audition for showman Billy Rose who was casting for a revue at the upcoming World's Fair. I reported backstage at the old Madison Square Garden together with over 200 other dancers, all attired in two piece outfits and tap shoes. I had put on my black leotard and tights as customary for most dance auditions. Seeing these masses of very beautiful girls with sexy outfits and heavy make-up, I lost all my confidence and decided not to even try to compete. Much to my amazement I found the next day a picture in the New York Times showing Mr. Billy Rose with one of the dancers he had picked, a pretty blond girl dressed in a black leotard, tights and ballet slippers! Another lesson learned in this amazing country! In show business one didn't give up without trying!"*

# CHAPTER 4 – THE CORLEY SISTERS

One early morning I reached into her collection for more memories, each one like the petals on her yellow rose, slowly opening, one at a time. She described a pivotal moment in her journey:

> *"My search for a job brought me to a theatrical agent. Waiting there was a young woman, also from Berlin, and looking for a job. Once again fate stepped in and brought us two refugees together. We decided to create a sister act, I took the name Joan and Marion became Mara. We were now the Corley Sisters."*

During my childhood, I often heard stories about the Corley Sisters. She selected the name Joan Corley because she admired movie star Joan Crawford. The last name came from the merging of 'Kroner' and Marion's last name 'Leiser' into 'Corley.' Years later, she chose Joan as my middle name:

> *"The NY Friendship House formed to help immigrants, gave us a rehearsal space and our act was born. Money was needed for costumes and photographs. My parents sold their wedding rings to buy the necessary materials and supplies. 'People know*

*we are married,' said my supportive mother, 'so the rings will help our daughter's future move, that is more important than proving our past!'"*

Another box revealed a packet of eleven postcards, handwritten in English by a twenty-year-old to her parents in 1940. They told a story of her efforts to follow a dream:

*"A few weeks later, we were introduced to George Scheck, a booking agent, later to become manager of singer Connie Francis...The first break; one week in Boston in a nightclub called the Silver Dollar. We scraped together our last few dollars and took the Greyhound to Boston, while four worried parents waved goodbye. Mara and I arrived in Boston with great confidence, expecting to see our names in lights within days, or weeks! The first paycheck was $65 of which the agent got 10% and our manager 5%. I had to send some money home to help my parents pay our rent and we needed some change to pay the bus fare to the next job in Lowell, Mass.*

*The club in Lowell had a big stage that rose from the dance floor to performing height. Very slippery and three shows a night. We organized ourselves for the essential tasks. I had to rehearse our music with the band and look after the costumes. Mara checked the dance floor and was in charge of our publicity. In every new city our photos had to be posted in the club and newspaper releases given. To make this simple, we pretended to really be blood-sisters and had to be very careful not to contradict each other in conversation. Mara was great in always covering up any discrepancies! Our agents still got their commissions, our parents the money for the rent, but we had a tough time making do with the rest of the salary. Usually our money ran out just before the last day and we would get paid between the second and third show of the final night.*

The Corley Sisters

*That didn't leave us much money for food but we were very happy. We began to be booked into better clubs, always for one week. One night we both were hungry and ran out between shows to have a dinner at a cafeteria. What would be cheapest and most for the money? Spaghetti of course! Only 35 cents for a huge bowl. We stuffed ourselves. Back to the club for the last show. One of our dances was a Russian dance...Final step; I had to lift Mara into a high jump and she would land on the floor in a split. Not on that night! Mara, plus a bowl of spaghetti stuck to that floor like glue! We both broke into a fit of laughter. Not a very good ending that night!*

*Finally, we were booked back into Boston. Our salary rose to $75 a week and between shows we would try to catch the stage show at the RKO or Loews movie houses where the Andrew Sisters and Abbott and Costello were headliners. Our agent assured us we would get into those shows soon. We worked extra hard and rehearsed new numbers, waiting for the big break. One night on stage, Mara twisted her ankle and was unable to perform for several weeks. We had to cancel all future bookings and return to New York. What a heartbreak and also financial disaster. In New York I did some solo club dates and we tried to improve our act. How about adding some songs?*

*Dance less and sing more! Enthusiastically we rehearsed the song, 'No. 10 Lullaby Lane,' singing one chorus and dancing the next one. We overlooked one fact, we were trained as good dancers but never learned how to sing! We undertook a crash course by Mara's uncle, an opera singer at the Met and then headed to our next booking in Worchester, Massachusetts! Our copy of the Andrew Sisters was less than spectacular. In the first show, we got so carried away that we sang and did some turns, knocking over the microphones in the process. We were cancelled after the first night and had to return to NY. One more try as singer-dancers in a New York City nightclub proved beyond any doubt that the Andrew Sisters did not have to fear competition from us! We scratched the songs and returned to our more successful dance format. One week in Plymouth, Massachusetts included a boat-ride from NY harbor to Plymouth for the entire cast which included a stripper with more luggage than anyone else!*

*During 1940 and 41, in one of my regular postcards to my parents I wrote, 'Our shows yesterday were very good and the mask dance a hit as usual. The boss asked us yesterday to change the dances so that the mask number is the last, because it is the best one. He seems to like us. We feel very happy working there.' Finally, our first stage show in an RKO movie house in Jamaica, Queens. We were closing in on Big Time. But once again fate stepped in. It was December 7, 1941. Sitting in the back seat, being driven back to NYC from a performance in the Catskills, the radio cut in with a special announcement; 'Pearl Harbor has just been bombed.' Mara and I didn't know where or what Pearl Harbor was and started to question our two drivers. Their explanations were quite confusing to us and we didn't know what to expect for the present and the future of our country, our lives, and indeed the future of the entire world."*

I leaned back in my recliner, pulled the red and blue woolen blanket crocheted by my grandmother around me and thought about how hard it must have been for my mother, an immigrant in America, just escaped from Germany to start a new life and career in America, suddenly swept up in the turmoil and fear of another World War.

One of my favorite stories was about the day she met my father. Her partner Mara's mother and a friend met at the popular Schrafft's restaurant in Manhattan. It was one of 34 in the New York area in those years. Their plan was for Mara and her to stop by, so a blind date could be arranged. My mother told me that a few weeks earlier, she visited a tealeaf reader. The woman glanced at her cup and declared, "You will meet a handsome man, with brown hair, and his name will begin with G." On December 11, 1941, a young man arrived at Schrafft's. He greeted her with the words, "What's your racket?" His name was Gustav Segal, he was tall with dark hair, and she remembered thinking that he looked like Cary Grant. About two weeks later, he proposed to her:

> "I broke the news to Mara that I wanted to get married. Mara proved to be a good friend and by the end of December our act ended following a week in Washington, DC. We'll never know if we would have made it onto the stage of Radio City. Eventually we both married, had children, and opened dance studios, grateful for the wonderful memories of our life as the Corley Sisters. Our friendship continued over 70 years."

I loved talking to Mara and she told about some of their professional experiences. During one of our phone conversations, she told me:

> "I studied only ballet and toe, your mother knew many other kinds of dance like character, so that helped us to put a performance together. We made our own masks and choreographed a dance to the song Moon Glow. The others were a Spanish on pointe and a Russian dance. I remember one hotel where we performed. The room had lots of holes in the walls. As I looked through one, there was another eye looking back at me!
>
> When she told me she wanted to get married, I accepted that because we were 'family.' We were both so young and went through a lot together. We were like the Bobbsey Twins, thought so much alike. That kind of friendship never dies."

Hannah and Gustav Segal

My parents' lives together began as America entered the war. Both were immigrants from Berlin who had escaped the Holocaust and fate brought them into a marriage that would last 49 years. My father often told me the story of how he came to America on a visitor's visa in 1936. When his year was up, his relatives told him not to return to Germany, that it was too dangerous. So he took a bus from New York City, traveled south on US One to Florida. A ship took him to Cuba where he spent a few days and was able to re-enter the United States. He started a neon sign business similar to the one he, his brother, and father had in Germany. His parents eventually were able to come to the United States and his brother emigrated to England.

And so on January 31st, 1942, my parents were married in a small ceremony. My mother described their honeymoon:

> "We drove a few hours and arrived in Lakewood, New Jersey. 'Where is our hotel?' I asked. 'I don't know,' said my new husband, 'I didn't make any reservations for just one night.' I tried hard not to show my disappointment. 'There are plenty of places

around.' The next hour was spent touring all hotels on Main Street, trying to find a room that was available and more important, affordable! Finally, we succeeded in finding a place that fit our small budget. Next morning, a quick breakfast and get ready to leave. 'Look at our car,' said Gustav, 'it got so dirty on the road, let's wipe it off.' I had never owned a car and was proud to have one now. So I thought, this was the thing one had to do, oblivious to the fact that I was well dressed for the trip home, not exactly equipped for a car wash!

The next morning, in our new apartment in Astoria, I made our first breakfast. Finding an old coffeepot on the stove, I quickly threw it out, replacing it proudly with a new, shiny percolator, a wedding gift from my mother. My husband protested, 'You don't throw anything out that you might still need some day!' In my haste, I forgot to put water into my new percolator when I put it on the flame and it was totally destroyed. I was reminded of this fatal decision by my husband during the 49 years of married life, whenever I wanted to get rid of any useless item!

A new dilemma arose after Gustav left for his job. I didn't know how to cook! My mother cooked a pot roast for us so I got on the subway to Washington Heights and brought it home for our first dinner. My husband was delighted and we were on the road to marital bliss! My friend Mara agreed to help with the next meal, we went to buy a chicken, all in one piece with the giblets inside. We washed it only on the outside, put it in the roasting pan. After a while a pretty bad odor drifted through my kitchen, and when my husband came home, we had to throw the chicken and the pot out, deodorize the kitchen and go out for a meal. We were both very happy the next day to welcome home my mother-in-law who was going to live with us and 'Hallelujah' cook our meals so I could go to work again and leave the stove to her!"

# PART II

# THE TEACHER

# CHAPTER 5 - ASTORIA

Soon my mother's career was destined to move into a completely different direction. World War Two raged on, as my parents welcomed me and my brother Gerald into their lives. My father now worked in a factory that made tanks for the war. As young children, we were oblivious to the hardships endured in our country during those years, especially for the newly arrived immigrants who struggled each day, and American citizens like the Japanese who were placed in internment camps in 1942. Even we were considered enemy aliens and had to give up our cameras, so there were few photos of me as a baby.

The long war ended in 1945. Two years passed. My mother wrote about a day that would once more change her life:

> "One afternoon, my new friend Carla said that she wanted to give her daughter dance lessons. I offered to teach her together with my own daughter in my living room. The green armchair became the barre for the four year olds to hold while they danced. This modest beginning attracted several children from the building and we outgrew my apartment. Carla suggested that I could actually start my own dancing school. A recreation hall in the basement on 33$^{rd}$ Street in Astoria, Queens was found; the first students came for one class a week. Music was a tambourine and windup Victrola. A few months later the landlord changed his mind so we found another recreation hall in an apartment building on 28$^{th}$ Street in Astoria. We painted, did the floor, got benches from the laundry room, a desk and curtains for the dressing room and office. My grandmother became the secretary. In 1947 the Hannah Kroner School of Dancing began."

The idea that American women in the 1940s could own and run a business was not something that happened too often. Before World War Two only 12 million worked, most white women stayed home. After Pearl Harbor, men enlisted as soldiers and workers were needed. Women who had been in traditional jobs like nurses and secretaries, became bank tellers and aircraft mechanics. After the war, public opinion began to change slowly. President Truman asked Eleanor Roosevelt to be the United States delegate to the new United Nations, this encouraged women to get more politically involved. The comic book character Wonder Woman appeared in 1941 as a feminist, giving women a heroine who fought for equal rights and encouraged growth in power. Despite the challenges that faced women in the business world at that time, my mother began a journey that would lead her in a new direction. Little could anyone imagine that her school would continue for more than 65 years, nor could anyone believe that thousands of children and adults would enter the world of dance my mother would create.

In a small box I discovered another packet of letters, a correspondence with her teacher, Max Terpis. In one of those letters, dated June 7th 1947, she wrote in German about the beginning of her school (translated):

> *My Dear Mr. Terpis, It is again time for a letter to you... The students love dancing and are so eager to learn. I switch between ballet and modern. So before I closed for the summer, we had a little recital to show the parents what the children had learned in the first three months. There was a bit of everything; the older ones showed a waltz, a march, pas de bourre and chaine...The show was such a big success with the parents and I was so proud that I sat down right away to write to you about it. In September I want to start classes again, hopefully already with more students, eventually I hope to open my own school. I got a lot of inquiries about tap dancing and since I did not feel secure enough to teach it, I went to school one more time... so, enough for today. I send you my good wishes and greetings from the whole family. A hug from your Hannah."*

I found many more letters between them until 1958 when Max Terpis passed away.

She wrote about one winter during those early years:

> *"There was a heavy snowfall, all the stores and schools were closed, but I had been trained that the show must go on! So I walked to our studio with Evelyn who was smaller than the mountains of snow, on my hand and I taught a class for one student who lived in the building and my daughter."*

She described her plans for her growing school:

> *"I was determined to give my pupils my all. Television was the new media so why not start there? I contacted the Dumont Network and an audition was arranged for my students to perform a dance suite of Disney characters. They wore masks that had a lot of white, which TV cameras couldn't photograph.*

*The color blue was used, but I could not transform Donald Duck into a blue faced duck, so we had learned an important lesson! I continued to pursue TV and met with success. The Ted Mack Amateur Hour and Paul Whiteman TV Teen Club chose my students and they performed on live television. There was one unexpected event before their performance, we found out that we were to follow a horse riding act and saw the horses doing what comes naturally during their act! Without any pause we got the signal to go onstage. It will be forever to the credit of the six girls that they danced their routine 'Stomping at the Savoy,' technically perfect and with smiles, ignoring the condition of the stage floor completely."*

Some of those first students, continued to dance for many years. Even after graduating high school, they stayed in touch. We enjoyed yearly reunions with this group over the decades. More recently, as we gathered in one of their homes, my mother told familiar stories about those first years. By now, her 'girls' were grandmothers themselves. We munched on cheese and crackers, listening to the memories of which we were all a part:

*"During those first few years in Astoria, there were yearly shows, the first in 1948, in a theater called Turn Hall. On the stage one of my students danced on a 'music box that started to tip during the dance. Undauntedly Pat did her turns and leaps on this dangerously wobbling platform while in the wings my heart was in my throat. But the show must go on was our motto and has been to this day.*

*Shows that followed took place at Hunter College in Manhattan. We insisted on a very professional atmosphere. I designed and sewed all the costumes myself. Parents were very supportive back stage, some became personal friends over the years. One year the theme was 'Museum' with pictures that came to life. Stepping out of the frame, Nancy Baron (a gifted young student) age eight, danced the little girl who was left behind as the museum closed and fell asleep in front of a painting of a*

*ballerina. The painting came alive in Nancy's dream and she
was allowed to dance a duet with the ballerina who then returned
to her frame. Nancy woke up and wistfully left the stage. There
was not a dry eye in the theater, when Nancy's big eyes turned
to the painting with that unspoken wish for the future.*

Hannah's Astoria Students

*An offer came to dance the Angels in Hansel and Gretel, as
performed by the Hunter College Opera Society. I choreographed
the piece for 12 girls. When we came to the stage, we saw that
a large rock had been placed on there. My Angels did their
dance formations as learned, but at certain moments my littlest
angel would disappear behind the rock and emerge only on the
next sequence. I should note that this young dancer and I
remained close* friends through the years."

In her notebooks there was a final tribute to her father:

*"It was his sense of humor that had let him come this far and
hopefully would keep him going for the rest of his life. Happily,
my dad lived to see me succeed in my chosen profession, get
married, and give him two grandchildren. He was as loving
and patient as their babysitter as he had been with me. We lost
my father in 1950, only 77 years old. The memory of his love
for me and my family has made my life much richer and made
me feel wanted and secure."*

Elsa and Eugene Kroner

## CHAPTER 6 - FLUSHING

I n 1952 fate brought changes once more as my mother lost the lease of her school. She decided to move to a new location, a store on Northern Blvd., in Flushing. Some of her students traveled by subway and bus from Astoria to continue dancing. As her school expanded she was determined to carry on her teacher's legacy to include story ballets performed in mime and dance. She drew from her training with Terpis and introduced her students to Greek mythology through stories such as *Circe* and *Niobe*. Interest in pantomime grew during the 1960s and 70's as she created several ballets including *Peter and the Wolf, Love for Three Oranges, The Flutist, Magic Spell, Animal Tales, and Trunk in the Attic*. Her students were challenged to create their own choreography, just as her teacher had done for her so many years before:

> *"Pantomime was different. Acting without words gave us a chance of building a character and course of action and becoming someone else through performance. Terpis knew that this technique was letting me be someone other than 'the only Jewish student in the school,' and promptly gave me solo parts in the pantomimes and ballets he created."*

Graduate Lorraine DiLandro remembered the ballets that my mother took her class to see in New York. "We came from homes where there wasn't the money for families to pay for tickets. One time Hannah took us to see Marcel Marceau. We studied his expressions to help us with our own pantomimes." The French actor mime Marcel was Jewish and when he was 16, had to flee from the Nazis during the Holocaust. He saved hundreds of Jewish orphans by telling them he would take them to the Alps on a vacation, eventually led them to Switzerland. Sadly, his father was murdered in Auschwitz.

It was during the 1960's in the Flushing studio that a special guest arrived. My mother's dance teacher Rolf Arco traveled to America for a reunion with her. She often told me stories about him, a nationally known professional dancer at the State Opera in Berlin. During the Hitler years, he was a fierce anti-Nazi who hid Jews, knowing that he could be arrested. After the war ended, he left Germany to live in Brazil. Now 30 years later, my mother proudly introduced him to her own students:

> "He watched my advanced jazz class, which worked as hard as never before and in which we all worked ourselves into such a pitch, that we applauded each other as I ended the class, after which they limped out exhausted and I had lost four pounds just in one day! There was very little comment from him on my work on that first day, but I was prepared for this since he always was a very demanding and strict teacher, and brutally honest. He still is! On Saturday he watched Evelyn's three classes and then my advanced ballet class. As a special surprise they did a polka for him which I originally learned from him. This he liked!" When we came home that day, he commented on Evelyn's magnificent teaching, and I was by then indignant enough to point out, that after all I had been her teacher! He looked at me in great surprise and declared that he had known me to be a good teacher 30 years ago, when I taught in his school, and that he had not expected me to get worse! However, Evelyn not being a professional dancer was much better than anyone had reason to expect!

*Then he got down to brass tacks! Why did my girls have stiff arms and did not use their heads properly? Being a practical man as well as a good friend and teacher, Arco set out right away to remedy the situation. Out of the trunk came a sweatshirt, old pants and loafers and the offer to teach my next Saturday class. When he stepped in front of them the next week, they were almost too scared to move, but as he started to work with them, all the magic of a seasoned performer and darn good teacher came through, and I saw my class dance, use their arms softly and improve so much in just one lesson, that it was unbelievable. They all fell in love with him. He taught three more times on Saturday...On the last Saturday he asked for music from the Polovetzian Dances, and proceeded to do a high leap with a double turn in the air! The magic of a profession one loves! The girls were in tears saying goodbye. On that afternoon, as we both came home tired, but happy, he admitted to me that he had found in my school the same atmosphere that we had in his school, that my work and school measured up to his highest expectations. The few weeks in my school had given him new energy, he was now going back to Brazil with a desire to work again and make dancing a part of his present life. It was the nicest thing he could have told me and so his visit helped us both more than anyone could have dreamed of."*

Rolf Arco and Hannah at Lincoln Center

During the following years, she introduced her advanced students to character dance as performed in ballets such as *The Nutcracker Suite*. Russian, Spanish, and Indian were some of the many dances that enriched their dance education. Whenever she began a dance she choreographed for them, she followed the example of her teacher, giving them a history of the composer, style, and whether it came from an opera, or ballet. In addition, they studied ballet, tap, and jazz as she had, attending several classes weekly. Performances were added in public schools, at libraries, even in department stores like Bloomingdales!

> *"At one of those shows a rousing finale music was interrupted by a dancer tripping over a wire backstage, thus stopping the tape recorder. Our well-trained cast of over 60 dancers continued their steps without music until we were able to plug in again. Music resumed and our dancers never lost a step to the end!*
>
> *At another performance a record player had been placed on a table on the wooden floor stage. As the girls started to dance, the vibrations of the floor made the needle on the record jump the grooves. Quickly I lifted the rather heavy Victrola off the table and held it in my arms for the next 30 minutes. The music was saved and so were the dances!"*

Then there was the Blackout of the entire city:

> *"...in the middle of a ballet class, New York City had a complete blackout. It caught us at the barre, music stopped, the studio became pitch black. On came my Eveready flashlight and we continued the barre work. A little later, my son Gerald came on his bike with an old army generator, which he set up and cranked for the next hour or more so we had enough electricity for music and one light. No one considered stopping the class."*

My mother's devotion to her students and determination was evident on another snowy morning in Flushing at 5AM, when my father shoveled out her car so that she could drive to the studio on Northern Blvd. Her mission was to give her student a warm up lesson before the audition for the High School of Performing Arts in New York City later that morning. At noon her pupil called with the news that she passed the audition. She went on to dance in the ballet company at Radio City Music Hall. That determination and discipline was emphasized during my mother's experiences in the Kulturbund during the Holocaust and passed on to her students.

Graduate student Bob Spiotto wrote, "I can still hear the sound of that dark brown wooden and glass door as you entered the studio in Flushing...The special care and attention she took in training and teaching cannot be measured." At each performance she gave him a very important job, it was to mop the stage before the show began, "...whether in the Temple basement, or on a temporary platform in Bloomingdales, packing and unpacking boxes of costumes, loading and unloading the big HK 'mobile,' and all that magical felt, the assorted props and the labeled cassette tapes. She was an inspiration- but to me was also someone I called teacher, advisor, supporter, fan, sounding board, mentor, friend, and family."

Carol Kaufman Riley, another student, was accepted into the Radio City Rockettes. In 1978, there was a memorable experience at that theater. My mother wrote:

> "Lassie was the headliner on stage and in his act a boy was chosen from the audience to come up and play a little skit with the dog. Carol had secretly arranged to have my grandson Ray Summer picked to come up on stage. Without blinking an eye Ray, eight years old, left his seat and went up where he played the scene and exited to good applause. Quickly our family went backstage. 'Ray,' I said, 'how did it feel to perform on this big stage in a famous theatre?' 'Oma,' was the immediate answer, 'I've been on stages before. This was not any different.' God bless the self-confidence of an eight-year old!"

Another example of her devotion to her students occurred on a Memorial Day weekend in the 1970s. Dance teacher and Parent

Sharon Wendrow remembered, "I was out of town and my daughter and Hannah's student Jill was staying at home with her older brother, Michael. She was there, because there was a rehearsal at the studio. Missing a rehearsal was never an option. At the same time, it was a holiday weekend, so Jill started the summer off with a day in the sun. A cooked lobster is pale by comparison to what she looked like. Hannah, knowing I was away, marched over to our apartment to minister to the unhappy girl and slather her with some kind of miracle lotion, so she would feel better. When HK came over and saw Jill, she looked at her, assumed her signature stance of fourth position, put her finger on her nose, also a signature move that we all knew and said, 'That wasn't very smart. Moving along.' And she never mentioned it again. At the same time, she gently lectured about the inadvisability of putting one's pale body in direct contact with hot sun for hours and hours, on the first time you sun bathed that year. HK also inquired as to what Jill was thinking doing such a thing right before a performance. Notice I said she marched over. HK never sauntered into a room. She never ambled along. She always strode into where she was going. She arrived with a purpose. You knew she was there, even if you weren't looking in her direction. A commanding presence. I know Jill must have had several different emotions that painful day, grateful and full of love that Mrs. Kroner cared so much that she came to her aid, nervous and guilty that she did something wrong and that Mrs. Kroner would be angry with her and relieved that she wasn't angry, just concerned about her well-being. This story is one of so many personal stories that show how thoughtful, caring, concerned, and loving she was to all of her students. She always went the extra mile, took the extra time, to make sure things were as they should be."

Hannah's Flushing Students

On sunny mornings in West Palm Beach, seated in our chairs under the palm trees, my mother told more stories. During those peaceful times the sound of seagulls and breaking waves gave us moments of reflection. She wrote about one of those times at the shore:

> *"It was afternoon and the sun started to go down. As the visitors were leaving, the seagulls started to move in. I noticed that they seemed to move in some form of groupings. Being a dancer and always thinking of new ways to choreograph a ballet, I decided to compose a group dance for my students called 'The Seagulls.' I was amazed how many different types of leaps, turns, slow and fast developed. It also inspired my students with ideas of their own to adapt their ballet technique to the movement of the birds on the sand. My stay at a beach turned into an inspiration for a successful performance at our next show."*

Always aware of the need to learn new techniques and ever changing styles, my mother joined The Dance Educators of America organization. She attended several meetings during the year together with close friend Dorothy (Dot) Winter, also a dance teacher, most held at the Waldorf Astoria hotel in New York. Well-known dancers were guest teachers. My mother was invited to teach at some of these meetings and brought her students to demonstrate the dances. Over the years several of her students entered competitions and took home top awards. She also taught character dance to beginning dance teachers at the summer training school. The ballroom was filled with about one hundred fifty students. The knowledge Hannah acquired from her teacher and experience in the Kulturbund was passed on to a new generation.

Since that afternoon in the living room in 1947, I also continued to dance. Just as she carried on her teacher's legacy, I emerged as a dance teacher to carry on her legacy. I created classes for three year olds, for boys, exercise for adults, and prenatal classes. I especially enjoyed assisting advanced students who themselves became teachers. Years later I became an elementary school teacher and staff developer on Long Island, while still continuing to teach dance classes at the studio.

Everyone in our family contributed in various ways to my mother's school. My father was the "official" painting decorator for our school. There was a decision to paint one wall pink and the other side green. That way the teachers could ask the students to "turn to the pink wall," or "the green wall!" For over 45 years, he continued to contribute his suggestions to her school. My husband Jerry whom I married in 1968, became her unofficial "musicologist." He suggested several pieces that she selected to choreograph dances to. One day he announced that he had a wonderful song for her. It was called "Doll on a Music Box" from the movie *Chitty Chitty Bang Bang*. "I have choreographed it for you, Mom," he told her. That evening in my parents' living room, he put on the record and did his dance for her. He spun around in a circle in slow motion, his hand over his eyes, to the verse, "What do you see," then lowered his arm, and raised it on his second rotation. When he came to the verse; "...waiting for love's first kiss," he blew kisses to all of us. My mother almost fell off her chair, laughing until tears rolled down her cheeks. "Now, I will never be able to do this dance, because I will always see you in my mind!" And she never did.

Evelyn and Jerry Summer

In 1977 she decided to expand to Albertson, Long Island, where former student and Radio City Rockette Carol Riley and I became the directors. Years later, Carol continued as owner. My mother's school also moved to Bayside, Queens where former teacher Sharon Wendrow became the owner and director. My mother taught advanced ballet classes in both locations for the next twenty years.

The world of dance that she knew in 1933 changed immensely over the years. In addition to ballet, tap, jazz, and modern, character, and pantomime, hip-hop, ballroom, lyrical and contemporary dance were added. Many studies have emerged to show that this activity can have profound positive effects. It can keep the body and brain active at all ages and help to develop self-confidence and self-esteem. Even at the age of 92 she enjoyed teaching, choreographing dances that were performed at yearly benefits, and passing on her legacy to new generations.

# PART III

# LEGACY

## CHAPTER 7 – RETURN TO BERLIN

T hroughout the years, the seashore remained a special part of my mother's life, and a source of stimulation for her choreography:

> "Looking out over the ocean gives me a sense of freedom and a feeling of connection to the countries on the other side of the 'the big water.' It makes me think of the past and of some old friends over there. Early in the morning the beach is still empty and very quiet. As the waves roll in, they have a rhythm of their own and suggest to me musical sounds and movements of dance. I seem to get more creative out there. Walking along... in late afternoon, the sun is slowly going down, causing the sky to get orange-red. The water seems to get darker and very peaceful. The end of another good day and a sense of gratitude and inspiration."

There was a special celebration in 1999 in our home. My husband Jerry lit the candle on a chocolate cake as our sons Ray and Dan looked on. Seated at the dining room table my mother took a deep breath and blew out the flame. "Sixty years ago this month, we left Holland and sailed to America." She explained that as they waited in Rotterdam

Holland, they were told that their ship was delayed. Another Dutch vessel, fully booked with no spaces for them, hit a German mine and sank in the English Channel. All passengers were killed.

In her notebook she wrote about those fateful days in 1939:

> *"The German newspapers printed the story and all our friends and remaining relatives in Berlin thought that it was our ship and that we had perished."*

As we finished eating the last cake morsels, her grandson Dan asked about her relatives. She said that the fate of family and friends still in Germany was a big worry. There was no communication for several years and they didn't learn what happened until long after the war ended:

> *"Lists kept by the Nazis of all the transports to concentration camps confirmed our worst fears. Except for my husband's brother and his family, everyone else was gone."*

Over the years, our family often thought about those whom we lost and especially on Yom HaShoah (Holocaust Remembrance Day). Both of my parents were always aware of how fortunate they were to have survived.

One day in 1992, my mother received an invitation to return to Berlin for a reunion of the Judische Kulturbund:

> *"Two free-lance journalists, one born in Germany, non-Jewish, and the other in Israel, Eike Geisel and Henryk Broder, authors of Premiere und Pogrom, came across some records buried in some Berlin archives, succeeded in finding and contacting former performing members who had survived and were still alive but scattered all over the world."*

I was invited to accompany her so we flew to Berlin on March 30th. An exhibit was created for the 44 survivors from various countries who attended along with family members. The German and foreign press, TV cameras greeted us as we arrived:

*"A lady ran toward me, arms outstretched and hugging me shouting, 'Hannah! I worked for you as a dancer. You were my choreographer in the last Ballet. I am Ellen Rathe.' It took a few embarrassing minutes for me to recognize her. Ellen told me that she had been unable to emigrate, stayed in Berlin all through the war, underground and without papers as a Jew, being hidden by friends, and lining up for some food and clothing whenever a big apartment house was bombed and the inhabitants lining up for relief rations, having lost their official ration cards in the air raid. Luckily she survived all the horror and still lived in Berlin."*

The stories of the Kulturbund were familiar to me, yet it was emotional to see my mother reunited with the artists from so many years ago, those who had survived and were still able to travel. This happened at just the right time, I thought. It was a onetime experience that we would remember for the rest of our lives.

One of the events we attended was a discussion of the Kulturbund with a panel that included my mother. The big auditorium, open to the public, was filled to capacity:

*"The six of us had worked at the theatre at different times, some until the bitter end at Westerbork concentration camp, deported but ordered to perform for the other victims. The panel spoke about whether performing at the Kulturbund was a good thing or not. An author, Herbert Freeden, who worked in the drama department of the theatre, felt that the artists were '... misled by our own leaders into a feeling of false security, that it was all an illusion...preventing many of us from seeking emigration.'"*

In the audience I listened as my mother spoke about her feelings, shared by the rest of the panel, that since she couldn't perform in any theaters in Germany, and it took a long time to receive the visa:

*"...I was happy to be employed by a professional theatre and to get my experience as a stage dancer and later choreographer...*

*it was not a happy time off the stage but it was constructive...to learn the theater arts; stage and costume design, direction, working with a big orchestra, etc. all of which came in handy in America. She added that the audiences were not permitted to visit regular theatres or movies, that there was no television as yet and on the radio only propaganda, and that my parents and friends always counted the weeks and days until it was their turn to come to our theatre and see an opera, musical, or a play.*

*In the middle of these two hours I had to almost leave the stage, quickly ate a cookie and hoped not to be asked a question while still chewing. Evelyn in the audience, held her breath at that point, if I'd make it through that evening, especially dealing with the painful past."*

A performance arranged for us all reflected her feelings about returning to Germany:

*"A film titled 'Lost in the Stars and Stripes' portrayed the life of a German Jewish emigrant, entering the United States at the time of Hitler Germany, getting used to a new country, language, lifestyle, and people, proudly becoming an American citizen, winning the war and later coming back to visit Germany with the thought of 'coming home,' only to find that it was not home anymore after all."*

We joined the group for a bus tour of the city:

*"Since the wall has come down, Berlin has become a very large city again and there was much to see. We spent the most time in East Berlin, which I had not seen since 1939. It is still in the most terrible of conditions except for a few show places, which the previous government had built to impress foreign visitors. The old buildings are falling apart, the effects of bombardment and shooting are still clearly visible on the houses that were left standing. Balconies have fallen off, and the openings are simply closed with wooden planks. The wall is*

*down, but so far nothing else has been built on stretches of the former no man's land. The elevated trains are unusable as are the tracks and overpasses. The East Germans renamed many streets for Communist heroes. Bombs also destroyed our theater and there was no trace of it anymore to be seen.*

*In West Berlin, luckily the buildings where I was born, my first school and my high school, had all survived and been rebuilt in the original style. This is what I wanted to show to Evelyn above all, and I was very excited for this chance. Nature has helped us to remember good times during childhood more clearly or maybe this is only true in my case, since I really had a very happy life before Hitler."*

After several other visits, it was time to say goodbye. She concluded:

*"It felt sad to close the book on the good times of childhood but it also felt good to 'go home now' and to our families across the ocean. Above all it made one feel humble, grateful to be alive, still stunned to be among the survivors of the Holocaust and determined to spread the word to the next generations that indeed it happened but it must not repeat history, God willing."*

Hannah in Berlin with writer Eike Geisel and dancer/survivor Ellen Rathe

Before we left Berlin, there was an unexpected event:

> "On the last morning I received a request for an interview.
> This reporter was writing for the PBS radio. I consented to give
> the interview.
>
> After that we returned to New York and a few weeks later I
> received a letter forwarded to me from the journalist in Berlin.
> It was from an Ursula K. Levy in Northridge, California, who
> wrote that she had read an interview in her local Jewish paper,
> it mentioned the name 'Kroner,' which was also her maiden
> name. As a Holocaust survivor she had lost all her relatives.
> Could it be possible that we were related?
>
> The name did not ring a bell so I answered the letter, but
> stated my grandfather's name, just in case. Well, by return mail
> came an excited answer. My paternal grandfather, Dr. Moritz
> Kroner of Berlin was one of the brothers of Ursula's grandfather
> Alfred Kroner. What an exciting discovery!
>
> I called this newly found cousin immediately, introduced
> myself and told her about three other Kroner cousins living
> in Massachusetts. We had survived the Hitler years and the
> war. It felt a little like the happy end of a fairytale. Kay's
> (Ursula) husband Fred created a geneology of our family on
> his computer, going back to 1700 in Germany and discovered
> additional relatives."

Over the next 15 years, we enjoyed several visits with the Kroner
cousins, their children, and grandchildren, a special gift from the
Kulturbund reunion.

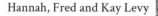

Hannah, Fred and Kay Levy

One of the family stories my mother told me was about her uncle, Dr. Karl Kroner. A neurologist. He was one of seven children of my great grandfather Dr. Moritz Kroner, and served in World War One on the French front. After the war ended, he was asked to see a patient in a military hospital who had gone blind.

Dr. Kroner examined him and gave his opinion that it was probably due to gas poisoning during the war and that this person would recover. That individual's blindness cleared up, as my great uncle said. The patient was Adolf Hitler. I learned from my mother's cousin Klaus that during the Holocaust, his father lost his medical practice and after being taken to a concentration camp, was able to escape with his wife and son to Iceland. In later years, we enjoyed many wonderful visits with Klaus, his wife Helen and their children in their home in Massachusetts.

One afternoon a short time ago, I opened one of my mother's notebooks and found another story about my grandmother, Elsa Kroner:

> "My mother had the ability to turn everything negative into a positive in our lives. My family lived in Berlin and although not super rich, we were comfortable and life was okay, until Hitler came to power. As German Jews, we had to deal with all kinds of losses; loved ones, our country, and many more. My mother turned the loss into a gain and set into motion all attempts to get us out of Germany while it was still possible to do so. We survived but had to deal with the loss of family and close friends as the war continued. I was still young enough to cope with the situation. She taught me that events that upset us enough to be considered a big loss, can turn out eventually to become a gain. My mother was right. Don't waste time feeling sorry for yourself. Accept your loss and go on with life in a positive spirit. Hope for the best!
>
> Once we were safely in America, she worked in a slipper place with piecework to supplement our income. Many years later in her eighties, she moved into an 'old age home.' She tried to do tasks in her new world, to make a little extra money, writing letters for people who needed help and teaching the cha-cha and rhumba to others. Her strength, willpower, and energy saved our family, a shining example for us all."

71

# CHAPTER 8 - REUNIONS

Recently, I opened a blue folder, inside were speeches she gave at the reunions of her school. At the 50th anniversary party in 1997 at a restaurant in Greenwich, Connecticut attended by approximately 100 graduates who had kept in touch, she expressed her amazement at this milestone:

> *"I didn't intend to teach just dancing! I hoped to teach a way of life. We were a school, but we also were family. Anything in your lives was of great interest and importance to me, and you returned that feeling. This is about friendship, love, loyalty, and trust...I lived, slept and breathed dancing, which my teachers gave me, to educate young people to move well, think, experiment and believe in themselves.*
>
> *Our school has produced many performers and teachers, as well as successful professionals in all fields of endeavor. Each year the Christmas cards of 'my kids' are displayed in my living room with great pride. Now the next generation is added on. Jackie and Krystal McCloy, working hard on their ice-skating career and taking classes with us, are the children of Lee Winter McCloy who studied with me in Flushing and taught*

*later with her mother, my very close friend Dot Winter. So we are teaching the third generation and still counting!*

*We are sharing the present, but also the past, which seems to become more important the older we get. After all, it is the past that has put down the foundation for the present and future."*

Our son Dan, 24 years old, spoke to the former students about his grandmother, he concluded by saying, "…Giving of oneself is so important and for fifty years my grandmother has done just that. Although I'm not a dancer myself, I feel that I was born to be in the arts and none of this would be possible without my grandmother. To be a creative person is one thing, to create for fifty years is another."

Our son Ray also addressed the group, "…Hundreds upon hundreds of performers have danced before me and never once was I to think that the ones on the Broadway stage were any more important than the ones in my grandmother's own studio. The fact that there are so many of us here lets me know that I wasn't the only one she imparted a love of theater to, and I know that all of you enjoy dreaming the same dreams as me." Sadly, his own dreams ended in October 2009 when he passed away at the age of 39, leaving his wife Courtney and daughter Olivia to carry on his legacy.

Hannah with her grandsons Ray and Dan Summer

My speech concluded with the following, "My mother opened the world of dance to me...I grew up to believe that through discipline, dedication, and the highest of standards, anything is possible...Today we celebrate fifty years of dance, friendship and love. We celebrate Hannah Kroner's life, a woman who has a loving and dancing heart."

One morning I opened an old cigar box that she had kept in her closet, it contained cards and letters that she kept throughout her life. One was from her student Judy Jablon:

*Letter to Hannah Kroner*
*About Sunday August 6, 2006*

*I woke up excited Sunday morning and as I drove out to Albertson on the Long Island Expressway I had the "I just can't wait" feeling that I so much associate with being a little girl.*

*And then, there we all were. A wonderful crew of Sunday morning dancers. Twenty-two of us who on the one hand have very different lives and experiences, yet on the other share the language of dance and a history of memories connected with Ms. Kroner. After some bubbly milling around and reminiscing in the lobby, we took our places on the barre and as if no time had passed, began to dance. We laughed, cheered, and thoroughly enjoyed ourselves from start to finish.*

*Sunday, dancing with you, Hannah, clarified for me once again why you are not only my first teacher (I started with you before I went to kindergarten,) but also my first mentor. What a master teacher you are. You are passionate about dance and teaching. And, you plan and adapt a lesson until, in this case, the night before, to ensure that the experience is respectful of and engaging for each of your students. And to be sure- the class was that and more for all of us. Thank you so much for the gift of a wonderful day.*

*And thanks to everyone who came. I can't wait until our next get together and hope that dancing together will be part of it. Driving back home I just kept smiling, which I continue to do as I recall the details of the day.*

*Judy Jablon*

On July 15, 2007, there was another reunion. It was the 60th anniversary of the Hannah Kroner School of Dance. We gathered together in a restaurant in Roslyn. Family, including our just married son Dan and his wife Margaret, about 100 graduates, staff, and friends from my mother's first school in Astoria, through to Albertson, shared this day. My mother spoke about the past 60 years:

> *"...I was determined to continue the teaching philosophy of my own teacher in Europe; 'Educate your students for all the demands of life, not only for the dance as an art form and entertainment, but body and brain to respond intelligently to any future situation.' I have followed this philosophy faithfully, through all the 60 years, as have all our teachers, and you are all here to prove us right!" Over the past 30 years, the Albertson studio has grown under the direction of Carol. I continue to enjoy teaching and choreographing in our school as well as being close to my family, which now includes a little great granddaughter, Olivia, two years old. And no surprise, she too has already learned that we keep dancing, wherever and whenever! To Evelyn, thank you for everything...and everyone here who is an important part of our 60-year history."*

Even at the age of 87 my mother led a rousing dance to the song, 'On a Wonderful Day like Today', her traditional warm up music, with all of us following her. As I looked at her I saw that she still lived to dance and danced to live. Her dream to create a school in 1947 and pass on her teacher's legacy came true. On that day my mother received the traditional bouquet of yellow roses.

Hannah and Carol

Dan and Margaret, Courtney and Ray

"Lift your right arm up high, stretch to the ceiling. Now lift your left arm. Take a deep breath, slowly lower your arms." About 15 men and women followed their teacher, some were in their nineties, a few were centenarians. Their teacher was Hannah Kroner in 2010, in the final chapter of her life. Every Monday morning at 10:30 she taught these seniors at the Bristal assisted living home she now lived in. The residents never missed a class, sitting on chairs waiting for half an hour before each lesson. Over the seven years she lived there, she declared to everyone, "I'm a working woman!" as she got into her car to drive to the dancing school and teach. I often stopped by with my two-year-old grandson Gus who danced with her in the lobby while her friend Murray played the piano.

Hannah with great grandchildren Olivia and Gus, and Evelyn

Hannah and Gus

She even choreographed a dance while listening to him playing and glancing at the large flower arrangement. Olivia also came to visit and enjoyed dancing with her great grandmother and a toy clown once sent to my mother by her former partner Mara. One afternoon I sat in the audience with over 50 residents to watch the show that featured staff and residents, who danced to a song choreographed by my mother, who also performed. Everyone applauded enthusiastically. A holiday show was performed by children from the dancing school, she bustled about, checking to make sure the dressing room, sound system, were all in order. It was a success. And so her legacy continued into her twilight years.

# CHAPTER 9 – HANNAH KRONER LEGACY

Years earlier the yellow rose given to her by her teacher long ago came to life again during a special visit with her friend in 1995:

> "I had kept in touch with Eva one of my dance classmates, who had emigrated to Switzerland. I followed her invitation for a visit to Zurich and we both had a wonderful time together in her little house on a hill with a lovely garden. We talked about the past and present and I admired her flowers, mostly red and pink roses. She admitted that yellow roses did not seem to do well in her garden...'Too bad,' I remarked, 'our teacher had loved them!' After a great week I was getting ready to leave. 'I wish our beloved teacher could hear how much we miss and remember him,' I said and walked down the hill to the garden gate. But then I stopped dead in my tracks! My last look at Eva's beautiful garden revealed among her pink roses <u>one big beautiful yellow rose!</u> It had suddenly appeared out of nowhere. Eva and I looked at this miracle then at each other, turned and walked away convinced that our beloved teacher was still with us, in our hearts and loving memories."

On a Sunday afternoon in 2011 she picked up a German language magazine. There was an ad. It read, "I may be looking for a needle in a haystack, I am an author and for my next project I would like to write about my street, Schwabische Strasse in Berlin. I hope that someone who knows that street will answer." So my mother wrote a letter to the author, Pascale Hugues:

> *"Maybe I am the needle in the haystack for you. My best friend lived on that street and we both went to the school on Barbarossa Platz. I was lucky to leave Germany with my parents in 1939 and go to New York, but my friend Susanne was a victim of the Holocaust. I am 91 years old, have children and grandchildren, but have never forgotten that time."*

Pascale answered, delighted to have found her. During the months that followed, she wrote letters and emails, asked questions about Susanne and my mother. I too assisted in her quest to write about her neighbors, present and past. My mother wrote about her friend:

> *"'Well,' said my girlfriend Susanne, 'If you are going to be ten days on an ocean liner, there will be social occasions for which you will need an elegant long evening gown! Let me make you such a dress.' Susanne made me a gorgeous, floor length black gown and matching jacket for the trip. I did wear it once on the ship and then kept it hanging in my closet for many years without a reason to wear it. My grandson Ray married Courtney, a lovely young lady and I gave her the black dress for special occasions. It fit her perfectly! As the years went on I forgot all about this dress."*

In 1939 when my mother arrived in New York, she was sure that Susanne would get her visa and join her. Sadly, that dream did not come true. Her best friend remained in Germany alone and fell in love with a Jewish man, born in Poland. They married and she was now listed with him under the Polish quota that had the longest waiting time:

*"The very sad ending of this story was that the war broke out, the remaining Jews were deported into concentration camps and killed. In Queensborough Community College nearby, one can see the German lists with the names of every Jew killed. I found my girlfriend Susanne's name on that list."*

As Pascale's visit approached, Courtney returned the dress to my mother. In April 2012, Pascale traveled to New York and came to Long Island to meet us. We welcomed her and showed her the dress so lovingly stitched by Susanne. My mother looked at her, "I think this would fit you!" A few minutes later, Pascale re-entered the living room wearing the black dress; it fit perfectly. "Keep it," my mother told her, "Take it back to Berlin, to Schwabishe Strasse where she lived. Then it will have come full circle."

Pascale Hugues wearing Susanne's dress

Together the three of us looked at old photos of the two friends so long ago, Pascale wrote several pages of notes. We drove to the dancing school where she looked at the photos on the wall of graduates of the school, watched and participated in a dance class for adults. During the following months she wrote about her progress; "I am now working very hard on my book...it has to be finished in mid-February...if all goes well, it will come out in August (2013.)...Susanne's dress is waiting in my wardrobe for the next occasion to be worn...

it is one of the most touching and saddest stories of the book. I consider it a big responsibility to write it as well as possible."

On September 20, 2013 Pascale emailed:

"I thought of you waking up this morning. Yes, the book is on the bookshop shelves and windows this morning! Tonight at 8PM is the very first reading...you will be sitting next to me in thoughts dear Hannah."

Her book, *Ruhige Strasse in Guter Wohnlage: Die Geschichte meiner Nachbarn*, (Quiet Street in a Good Neighborhood: The Story of my Neighbors) was published, first in German and then in French, *La Robe de Hannah* (The Dress of Hannah.) In the chapter about my mother and Susanne, she wrote about their lives in Berlin so long ago; two best friends, who played together, had birthday parties, laughed, and enjoyed their lives, until it was all taken away. In an excerpt, (translated from German) Pascale wrote:

> "The year is 1939 and Hitler declared war two months ago. The Kroners sell all their furniture in order to be able to buy tickets for a passage to America. Eugene Kroner buys three one-way tickets on the S.S. Rotterdam to New York. Hannah and her friend Susanne fantasize about the glamour on the ship and Susanne sews a gorgeous ball gown for Hannah to wear onboard. 'A beautiful dress. I did wear it on the ship. And later, when I went out with my husband. When my baby was born, it didn't fit anymore.' Hannah stored the dress with the memories of Susanne deep in her closet....74 years later Hannah talks to me...'There is only one who can wear this dress-you! And I would feel happy if you take it and bring it to where it belongs, Susanne's street. Maybe you would wear it sometimes to revive memories that it evokes? Please take it...the dress has outlived the person.' I feel a bit intimidated in this 74-year-old dress. It needs to be ironed and shortened, but it is perfect... I return to Berlin and send Hannah a picture of myself in the dress on my balcony.

I wear the dress. One day I find an email from her '...You look so great on the balcony in the street where Susanne lived, and I feel very strongly that this dress must stay with you and not in a museum where one sees it but doesn't understand the circumstances.'" (Pages 136, 147)

At the European Parliament in Brussels, on December 3, 2014, Pascale was awarded the European Book Prize for her book, translated into French and titled, *La Robe de Hannah*. In her acceptance speech, she said:

> "The story would not have been possible without the courage of my neighbors who all with whatever pain or horror they had experienced, agreed to tell me their lives... Jews and non-Jews, the inhabitants of the early century until my current neighbors from 1904-2014. The book "...tells the story of the dress that Susanne, Hannah's best friend, who was also Jewish, sewed for Hannah before her emigration to the United States. Hannah survived. Susanne was exterminated in a camp. When I sent my book to Hannah...she replied, 'My friend Susanne remains unforgotten. I feel good that this dress stays in your street. Please wear it, Susanne can rest in peace. Me too. And in a book, for one dress to make a world trip and return 70 years later that should be a good theme...' Pascale concluded, "I feel tonight that Hannah had lots of intuition! Thank you."

Last Fall, my ten-year-old granddaughter and I walked down the marble steps at Lincoln Center after the dancers took their last bows. "I loved the first ballet the best," said Olivia. "Why," I asked her. "Well, Omi, that's because the dancers wore purple!" My mother would have loved her response. Over so many years, it was my mother and I who sat in the plush red seats ready for the lights to dim and the curtains to part. On this October afternoon in 2015, it felt different, as my mother passed away this summer. I wanted to carry on the tradition that she began when I too was ten years old.

Hannah and Evelyn

Great granddaughter Olivia at
Lincoln Center

On a recent Saturday morning, my granddaughter Olivia and I pushed open the door to the dancing school. My mother's great granddaughter entered her weekly jazz/hip-hop class. With my computer in my hand, I walked into the dressing room on the other side of the wall, sat down and opened to the story of my mother's life. I continued to write as I listened to the sounds of her teacher Heather, who was one of my mother's former students, the music, and Olivia's classmates who worked to learn the new steps.

Olivia at the Hannah Kroner School
in Albertson

Yellow roses for Hannah from the students

Was it so long ago that I stood next to the green armchair in our living room, tried to place my small feet into a first position. Had we come full circle almost 70 years later? What did it all mean?

My mother brought with her a history of survival; her teacher and mentor Max Terpis, best friend Susanne, boyfriend Vimms, theater performances in the Kulturbund, fled the country she was born in and began a new life and career in America. She took those experiences into her dance studio, where she nurtured children for over 65 years. Several of her students looked at her as a second mother, were inspired, felt safe, developed confidence, and grew up to bring her gifts to the next generation, and the next. At Christmas and Chanukah, she placed over a hundred cards on her dresser from her students with notes that included: "I am a teacher because of you." "Your love for dance ignited a passion so deeply within me that I continue to pass along your teachings, technique, and respect for this beautiful art…" "You raised the bar for us as a class and individuals to become the best dancer. You recognized where our strengths lay and helped us grow…" Graduates remembered her with letters, phone calls, lunches, and reunions. There was a celebration at the end of each decade. They brought their children and grandchildren to meet this special teacher. traveling from New York, Florida, California, and other states.

During her 95 years, my mother was part of the incredible history of the twentieth century world. An invisible wall descended on her in 1933, stole her family's freedom, created fear and terror for many. A wall imprisoned her friend Susanne inside, left her to perish. My mother and her parents emerged through a small opening in that massive wall to sail out of darkness into the light. World War Two finally ended. Almost two decades later, a new wall arose, separating families in East and West Germany. She returned to Berlin in 1992, after that wall was torn down and the country reunited.

The wall my mother built, brick by brick, stands strong, a wall of discipline, commitment, persistence, it lifts us all. It still remains, passing on her legacy to those who continue to join this family. She had a priceless impact on thousands of her students, friends, and family. Broadway, dance companies, theater directors, psychologists, and teachers were some of the professional careers they achieved. Her legacy lives on through the lives she touched. As her daughter, I feel that she gave me footprints to follow by her example, the tools to pass on to others. Her talents were exceeded only by the courage she showed through the curves in the roads. Above all, it was the love of her profession that kept her going.

My mother passed away in the summer of 2015 at 95 years of age. She told me, "I had my career, my family, and friends. I did it all. So when it's time, I will go and feel that I had a wonderful life."

## "The Four Big L's
## <u>Written by Hannah Kroner</u>

*Live your life to the fullest,*
*And don't have any regrets*

*Love what you do,*
*And are able to achieve*

*Learn something new,*
*Every day of your life*

*Laugh at the world,*
*And it will smile back at you.*

# EPILOGUE

In the spring of 2016 I returned to Berlin, this time with my ten-year-old granddaughter Olivia. Together we traced the footsteps of my mother's childhood, her school, the zoo, her house, the town hall, and Schwabishe Strasse where her friend Susanne lived. Author and friend Pascale drove us to my mother's elementary school. Nearby was a yellow wall of bricks. Students wrote the names of Jewish children who attended that school during the Holocaust and were murdered in concentration camps. As we walked slowly along the wall, I spotted the name 'Rosa Wachsner.' Her last name was the same as my mother's girlfriend Susanne. It may have been her cousin.

Olivia in front of my mother's school

Holocaust victims' names written by children in the school

After that, Pascale took us to the Weissensee Cemetery which is the second oldest Jewish cemetery in Europe. Olivia noticed the stones at the entrance, each marked with the name of a concentration camp. She picked up a stone and placed it on the one that said, 'Bergen Belsen.' "That is where Anne Frank died," she told me. Inside the building, we approached a young man and I asked if he could locate my great grandparents, Dr. Moritz Kroner and Emily Frenkel. He turned to a computer and within a few moments found their graves. "You may not be able to read their names on the stone." With a map, we began our walk through history.

After about half an hour, we came to the corner that the map indicated. At first there was no sign of the grave. "Here it is," called Pascale. There it was with the name 'Kroner' at the top of the tall stone structure. Although covered with vines and bushes, both of my great grandparents' names were visible. We read that he was a doctor who treated the soldiers in World War One. "Olivia," I said, through my tears, "here are your great great great grandparents!" Nearby was a field with small stones, hundreds of Jewish soldiers who died fighting for Germany in the First World War.

My great grandparents' graves

On a sunny morning Ingeborg Geisel, widow of the writer Eike who reunited my mother with survivors from the Kulturbund, drove us through the streets of Berlin. New modern buildings reflected the robust city. "Here is where the wall stood," she pointed out. That wall divided East and West Berlin from 1961 until November 9th, 1989. Now, it was a united city once more.

There was one special place that I wanted to show Olivia; Kadewe, a large department store on the Kurfurstendamm Strasse. Up on the roof was a restaurant with delicious desserts that my mother often told me about. During the Holocaust, when Jews were not allowed into that building, my mother's nanny who was not Jewish, took her there, being careful not to be noticed. Now it was my turn to bring Olivia there for dessert. 80 years later my mother's great granddaughter sat in Kadewe and dipped her spoon into her chocolate pudding. The circle was closed.

Chocolate pudding at Kadewe!

# GLOSSARY

**Anti-Semitic**- Hatred of Jewish people

**Boycott**- refuse to use or buy a product, way to protest

**Concentration Camp**- A place that imprisons large amounts of people, may include forced labor or mass execution. Several hundred camps were created during the Nazi Holocaust including Auschwitz, Dachau, and Bergen Belsen

**Final Solution**- The Nazi plan to annihilate or murder the Jewish people, decided in Wannsee, near Berlin in January 1942 after a decade of discrimination

**German Reich**- German word that means empire. The Third Reich referred to Germany during the Hitler years

**Holocaust**- The period of time from 1933 when Adolf Hitler was the chancellor of German to May 1945 when World War Two ended. During those years 6,000,000 Jews were murdered

**Paul Hindenburg**- President of The Weimar Republic in 1925. He appointed Hitler as chancellor in 1933

**Pearl Harbor**- Japanese fighter planes bombed the naval base near Honolulu, Hawaii on December 7, 1941, which caused the United States to enter World War Two

**Nuremburg Laws**- At a rally held in Nuremburg, Germany in 1935, new laws were enacted that discriminated against Jews

**Refugee**- Someone who flees to a foreign country due to fear of persecution because of religion, nationality, race, or for political reasons

**Rescuers**- Ordinary people who helped primarily Jews by hiding them, leaving food, assisting them to emigrate. They include American Varian Fry who rescued artists and writers in France, Miep Gies who hid Anne Frank and her family, Raoul Wallenberg a Swedish diplomat who saved thousands of Hungarian Jews, and hundreds of other courageous individuals

**Treaty of Versailles** - A peace document signed in 1919 at the end of World War 1

**Yom HaShoah**- means complete destruction in Hebrew. It refers to World War Two and the atrocities that were perpetrated against the Jews. It is a memorial day for those who perished in the Shoah, also known as the Holocaust

**Weimar Republic**- Constitution adopted by Germany at Weimar in 1919

# ACKNOWLEDGMENTS

**A most appreciative thank you to:**

**Irving Roth**, Director of The Holocaust Center at Temple Judea, Long Island, for his inspiration and assistance to bring the manuscript to completion.

**Jill Wendrow Ankermann**, Graduate, Board Member of The Hannah Kroner Legacy Foundation, for her intelligent guidance and love.

**Bob Spiotto**, Graduate, Board Member of The Hannah Kroner Legacy Foundation, who inspired the writing of this story.

**Lee McCloy**, Graduate, Board Member of The Hannah Kroner Legacy Foundation, who lovingly assisted in the creation of this foundation.

**Dr. James Muyskens**, former President of Queens College, for his guidance, wisdom, and patience in the revision of the manuscript.

**Friends, Students and Graduates of the Hannah Kroner School of Dance**, for their love, friendship, and encouragement over so many years.

**Judy Jablon**, Graduate, whose experience as a writer and educator gave me the courage to tell my mother's story.

**JoAnne Gaffney Greenbaum**, Graduate, who opened her home, read numerous drafts, and provided inspiration for the revision of the manuscript.

**Courtney, Dan, Gus, Jerry, Margaret, and Olivia Summer**, for their unconditional love and inspiration.

# BIBLIOGRAPHY

Geisel, Eike, and Henryk Broder, eds. *Premiere und Pogrom: Der Judische Kultur-bund, 1933-1941, Texte und Bilder.* Berlin: Siedler, 1992.

Hugues, Pascale. *Ruhige Strasse in Guter Wohnlage: Die Geschichte meiner Nachbarn.* Germany: Rowahlt, 2013.

Hugues, Pascale. *La Robe de Hannah.* Paris: Les Arenes, 2014.

Hugues, Pascale. *Hannah's Dress.* Cambridge, England: Polity, Spring 2017.

# ABOUT THE AUTHOR

Evelyn Summer grew up listening to her parents' and grandparents' stories about their lives in Germany before and during the Holocaust years. As a graduate of NYU and Hofstra University, those stories traveled into the school classrooms on Long Island, including Oceanside, where Evelyn taught children for over twenty-five years. Teachers College, Columbia University, gave her the opportunity to refine her writing skills which she shared with teachers as a Staff Developer in various school districts throughout Long Island. She gathered new stories, creating memoirs and poetry. The dance education she received from her mother as a student and teacher contributed to her love of the arts.

CONTACT INFORMATION

Email: Hannahkronerwekeepdancing@gmail.com

Website: hklegacy.org

Evelyn lives in Queens, New York with her husband Jerry. Their lives were enriched with two sons; Ray and Dan, and grandchildren Olivia and Gus.

# THE HANNAH KRONER
# LEGACY FOUNDATION

Evelyn Summer is the President of The Hannah Kroner Legacy Foundation created together with several dance graduates from the school Hannah Kroner founded. The mission is to preserve and celebrate the passion of one dancer's unique journey from persecution during the turbulent 1930's in Berlin, to a world that offered her the freedom and opportunity to create a lasting legacy.

- This non-profit organization plans to fund higher education scholarships for aspiring deserving students of dance and musical theater
- Educational initiatives will provide resources for schools, religious institutions and programs in the community
- Performances and projects will carry on the legacy of Hannah Kroner

"Mrs.Kroner once came to see me perform the Nutcracker and told me how proud she always was to see her students performing. She said we were all her 'seeds' and that she loved to watch us bloom. I will always continue to spread her wisdom, knowledge, and love for dance in my studio! My students are still part of her beautiful garden! So I will continue to sprinkle and nurture them just as she did for us."

—*Mary Delano Negron,*
*Graduate student*